Sheffield Hallam University
Learning and IT Services
Adsetts Centre City Campus
Sheffield     S1 1WB

101 841 075 9

# Markets as sites for social interaction

D1628036

SHEFFIELD HALLAM UNIVERSITY
LEARNING CENTRE
WITHDRAWN FROM STOCK

This publication can be provided in alternative formats, such as large print, Braille, audiotape and on disk. Please contact: Communications Department, Joseph Rowntree Foundation, The Homestead, 40 Water End, York YO30 6WP. Tel: 01904 615905. Email: info@jrf.org.uk

# Markets as sites for social interaction

**Spaces of diversity**

Sophie Watson *with* David Studdert

First published in Great Britain in September 2006 by

The Policy Press
Fourth Floor, Beacon House
Queen's Road
Bristol BS8 1QU
UK

Tel no    +44 (0)117 331 4054
Fax no   +44 (0)117 331 4093
Email    tpp-info@bristol.ac.uk
www.policypress.org.uk

© The Open University 2006

Published for the Joseph Rowntree Foundation by The Policy Press

10-digit ISBN 1 86134 925 4
13-digit ISBN 978 1 86134 925 5

British Library Cataloguing in Publication Data
A catalogue record for this book is available from the British Library.

Library of Congress Cataloging-in-Publication Data
A catalog record for this book has been requested.

**Sophie Watson** is Professor of Sociology and **David Studdert** is a research fellow, both at The Open University.

All rights reserved: no part of this publication may be reproduced, stored in a retrieval system, or transmitted in any form or by any means, electronic, mechanical, photocopying, recording or otherwise without the prior written permission of the publishers.

The **Joseph Rowntree Foundation** has supported this project as part of its programme of research and innovative development projects, which it hopes will be of value to policy makers, practitioners and service users. The facts presented and views expressed in this report are, however, those of the authors and not necessarily those of the Foundation.

The statements and opinions contained within this publication are solely those of the authors and not of the University of Bristol or The Policy Press. The University of Bristol and The Policy Press disclaim responsibility for any injury to persons or property resulting from any material published in this publication.

The Policy Press works to counter discrimination on grounds of gender, race, disability, age and sexuality.

Cover image kindly supplied by Karin Cameron
Cover design by Qube Design Associates, Bristol
Printed in Great Britain by Latimer Trend Printing Group, Plymouth

SHEFFIELD HALLAM UNIVERSITY
ADSETTS LEARNING CENTRE
WL
307.333
WA
LS

# Contents

# Acknowledgements

I would like to thank the Joseph Rowntree Foundation for funding the project. I would also like to thank the following people for their contribution to the research: Anne Jungman, Eva Kekou and Rosemary Pringle for helping when needed; and particularly Katharine Knox for her insightful, detailed and helpful comments on the report. Margaret Marchant's administrative help was, as ever, invaluable. I would also like to thank the following members of the project advisory group who shared their expertise and knowledge of markets, and advised us when needed: George Nicholson, Kris Zasada, Simon Quin, Theresa McDonagh, Gary Bridge, Tim Butler, Mica Nava and Karim Talal. Graham Wilson from the National Association of British Market Authorities and Nicholas Rhodes were also generous with their time and knowledge. Finally, I would like to thank all the council officials, traders and shoppers who were interviewed for the research.

The photographs in the report were all taken by the researchers.

# Executive summary

This project was set up to explore the importance of markets as social spaces in towns and cities in the UK. Despite some local variation, many local retail markets have been in decline over the past 20 years. Typically, they have suffered from a distinct lack of investment, with local authorities choosing to finance capital programmes in services that are deemed to be a higher priority, such as education, housing and social services (NABMA, 2005). Many markets therefore look tired and run down, and the facilities are poor. Despite a large increase in the number of stalls available from 1998-89 to 2003-04 (with 3,911 additional stalls, raising the total available to 150,000 across the UK), there has been a significant fall in occupancy rates in the same period – from 79% to 75%. Footfall levels have also fallen: in 2000-01, total weekly visits stood at 5,473,955; this fell to 5,363,437 shopping visits per week in 2003-04 (NABMA 2005).

At the same time, particularly over the past decade, there has been a steady growth in the success of specialist niche markets: farmers' markets, craft markets, Christmas markets, French and German markets, and, in London, Borough Market (*The Economist*, 2003). For example, it was reported that from 1998-99 to 2003-04 there was a 250% increase in farmers' markets and a 233% increase in stalls, and that shoppers visiting these events increased by 574% (*The Economist*, 2003). To what extent this trend represents a long-term shift in consumer preferences is hard to assess. However, it indicates that the popularity of the market per se is by no means in decline, and that markets can offer possibilities not just for local economic growth but also for people to mingle with each other and become accustomed to each others' differences in a public space – thereby acting as a potential focal point for local communities that could revitalise public space.

This report aims to consider the role of markets as social spaces. In particular, it explores the importance of markets for different groups in society, and the forms of interaction enacted in market sites. Eight markets were selected to reflect:

- different kinds of markets: covered and uncovered; detached from, and attached to, shopping centres; street markets and markets located in town centres;
- different sociodemographic and economic contexts in terms of local population profiles;
- different locations: metropolitan, urban and rural.

Interviews with shoppers, traders and local officials (including town centre managers and council staff involved in managing local markets) were conducted in these sites, and in-depth observation was carried out (along with photographic records) in order to identify the crucial factors that affect the success of markets as social spaces. This locally based information was supplemented by in-depth interviews with key national informants on markets in Britain.

The findings indicated that markets are indeed important sites of social interaction for local communities. Although the markets in the study varied considerably in the level of social interaction, the strength of social ties, the level of social inclusion and the use of the market by different groups, in all the markets some degree of social interaction took place and in most cases respondents confirmed the significance of the market as a social space.

The report concluded that for a market to function well as a social space various factors were significant in varying degrees. Essential attributes were as follows:

- **features to attract visitors to the site** – including a diverse range of products that made a good 'fit' with local community needs and 'tastes', and a sense of surprise or the unexpected to provide interest;
- **opportunities to linger** – café(s) or food van(s) on site or close by were key here – informal seating areas could also be important though less critical;
- **good access to the site** – public transport was key but opportunities to come by car and access to parking were also important for some visitors;
- **an active and engaged community of traders** – both to provide the retail offer but also to provide part of the social life of the site itself.

Other important, but less essential, attributes were as follows:

- **a well laid out site** – with thought given to the layout of the stalls, linchpin stalls or features (the café often being one) and particular features such as roomy aisles for people to walk through easily, as well as protection from the weather in more open sites;
- **connection with other retail outlets** – to ensure the market was embedded in the local retail offer;
- **effective management of the site** – and a leadership role from councils to provide a strategic direction for the market.

The report concludes by underlining the potential role of markets to act as a significant site of social interaction for a community. It argues that the lack of policy and strategy for markets at a national level should be addressed, and that markets could potentially play a key role in wider policy agendas, such as policies addressing social exclusion or healthy eating. It also suggests that the place of markets in community development and local regeneration policies should be strengthened. Given the evident success of farmers' and other specialist markets, and also of many other more traditional markets in British towns and cities, both economically and as social spaces, the report argues that their provision in local areas should be encouraged. Most importantly, market provision in any one locality needs to fit with, and be responsive to, the surrounding community needs, socioeconomic and demographic profile, and local conditions.

# Markets in context

## Introduction

Markets have a very long history and have been key focal points in the centres of British towns and cities for as long as they have been in existence; indeed, many towns are still known as 'market towns'. As such, they have represented important public spaces. Despite their traditional significance as sites of commerce, consumption and social interaction, more recently a narrative of the decline of markets, with the exception of farmers' markets and specialist markets (for example, Christmas markets, French and German markets and – in London – Borough Market [*The Economist*, 2003]), is more commonly heard. Over the past 20 years, a number of markets across the country have been under threat, closed down or resituated. According to Simon Quin (Towns Centre Initiative), markets were thriving in the mid-1980s. The fact that markets were largely found to be profit making through to the mid-1980s gave rise to a generalised growth in provision, in particular an increase in market days and projects, on the mistaken assumption that the same level of demand would continue (Simon Quin interview).

If markets traditionally have represented key public spaces in cities, does their economic decline in some localities necessarily imply a diminution in their role as social spaces also? This study asks: What are the key factors that make a market work well as a social and vibrant public space for different groups in the community? Who are the main users of markets as social spaces? What are the different kinds of social interaction in a market?

First, a brief overview of the wider policy context is relevant here.

## Policy context

As a result of sustained pressure from interested individuals and groups such as the National Association of British Markets Authorities (NABMA), when the government issued its new planning policy for town centres in March 2005, this encouraged authorities and developers to create the right space for markets in towns and cities:

> Street and covered markets (including farmers' markets) can make a valuable contribution to local choice and diversity in shopping as well as the vitality of town centres and to the rural economy. As an integral part of the vision for their town centres, local authorities should seek to retain and enhance existing markets and, where appropriate, re-introduce or create new ones. Local authorities should ensure that their markets remain attractive and competitive by investing in their improvement. (ODPM, 2005)

Overall, however, national policy on markets has been relatively weak and uncoordinated, falling between a number of different departments with their respective agendas and remits. Currently, the Department for Environment, Food and Rural Affairs (DEFRA) and the Department for Communities and Local Government (DCLG) (formerly the Office of the Deputy Prime Minister, or ODPM) are the main departments with an interest in markets, but there is no clear or coordinated overall policy direction. In

DEFRA's case, the focus is on wholesale food, agricultural products and livestock markets, rather than more general markets. The DCLG's policy agendas are potentially of greater relevance to markets, particularly policies focused on town centre regeneration or the sustainable communities and social exclusion agendas, but to date markets have not been considered as a key site for intervention. There is, though, considerable potential for markets to play a significant role in these and other areas, such as the healthy food agenda and tackling obesity in children. Currently, resources to support markets are allocated through Regional Development Agencies and Countryside Agency programmes, which are aimed at market town regeneration, but markets per se are not the key focus and other support for markets is often limited to staffing and other provision from councils, which, in many cases, continue to manage the sites that they have historically owned.

## Markets as public spaces

Despite growing government interest in public space – illustrated in publications such as the Urban Task Force's report *Towards an Urban Renaissance* (1999) and the Urban Greenspaces Task Force's *Living Places: Cleaner, Safer, Greener* (ODPM, 2003) – there is a relatively limited amount of research to date on how social relations play out in public space across different groups (defined here by gender, age, race, ethnicity and socioeconomic position) or on how public space is perceived and used. More specifically, the role of markets as public spaces has also been ignored.

In the academic field, there is now a considerable body of work that theorises the public realm, from Habermas' notion of the public sphere as a site of rational debate and communication (Habermas, 1984) to Young's notion of the city as a space for 'the meeting of strangers' and as 'a community of difference' (Young, 1990). Other literature on the public realm has tended to focus on the decline of the public realm and privatisation of social relations (Sennett, 1974, 2000) or on public spaces as sites of contestation or conflict – such as Smith's work on gentrification (Smith, 1996) or Kaznelson's work, which introduces the notion of the disenfranchised occupying 'city trenches' (Kaznelson, 1981). Sennett, for example, notes that, for many in the city, the unpredictability of encounter can result in conflict or a pervasive feeling of threat (Sennett, 1974). Others have also highlighted the ways in which urban space is being increasingly privatised or withdrawn (Sorkin, 1992; Mitchell, 1995, 2003). At its most extreme, the privatisation of public space becomes fortress-like and militaristic as private interests exert literal or symbolic violence on those urban residents whose presence unsettles economic interests (Davis, 1990). Hitherto, open and uncontrolled public spaces of a city, sites of unpredictable encounter, have either been made subject to controls and surveillance or made into semi-privatised spaces. The power of private capital to thematise and commodify these spaces as sites of consumption further degrades the opportunity for idling, casual mutual performance and display and chance engagement. Urban spaces have been 'Disneyfied' (Sorkin, 1992).

What is missing from these accounts are the day-to-day explorations and understandings of how different groups interact, or not, in public spaces when these are not overtly conflictual. We still know remarkably little about how different people actually live together in different public spaces of the city, despite the meta-narratives of the public realm or public space. Yet, one of the key aspects of the contemporary city is the living of difference in the context of intense juxtaposition and social connection (see Massey et al 1999). Some writers celebrate the city as a site of difference, seeing this as providing new possibilities for democratic communities (for example, Young, 1990), while others see the diversity of the city as leading to over-stimulation and hence the need for retreat (for example, Simmel, 1903a, 1903b, 1903c).

This study sets out to help fill these gaps on how people use public spaces, building on the few existing studies to date (Deutsche, 1996; Fincher and Jacobs, 1998), including the author's previous exploration of urban encounters in marginal and symbolic public spaces (Watson, 2006). It sets out to consider the humdrum or everyday cultural practices that form much of the texture of daily urban life, focusing on markets.

As one of the key sites of public space in the city, markets take many different spatial forms: outdoor markets – both covered and uncovered, indoor markets, street markets and markets attached to shopping centres. They also vary in terms of the range of products sold and in their size. In some cases, markets comprise as little as 20 stalls, while elsewhere there are closer to 200 stalls. Typically, markets are run by local authorities, although there is a growing number of markets run by private companies, community-run markets, farmers' markets, and private and public partnerships.

In many cases, markets act as a focal point for the locality and as a hub of connection, interconnections and social interaction, and many markets have a very long history. How successful they are as sites of sociality has not been explored, although, in recent years, a narrative of the decline of the older-style street markets, and the apparent success of the newer farmers', specialist and organic food markets has become common in the press. Why some markets are thriving and others are in decline is not easy to pinpoint, though a complex interrelation of factors can have an impact, such as the growth of the local supermarket as a competitive alternative and the redevelopment of market sites by private developers, leading to the relocation of markets to new sites – indoor and outdoor – away from the market's traditional constituency. Yet, markets can offer possibilities not only for local economic growth but also for people to mingle with each other and become accustomed to each others' differences in a public space; in this way, markets can act as potential focal points for local communities. As sites of public interaction and retail spaces, where traders pay rent for their stalls, they could in some senses be described as public/private spaces, disrupting the often rather rigid and ill-conceived boundary between public and private space.

The limited research on markets has mostly been undertaken overseas and has focused on the economic aspects of markets. For example, Sherry's (1990) ethnographic case study of a mid-western American flea market looked at market buyer and seller behaviour, market place ambience, the social embeddedness of consumption and experiential aspects of consumption. Bromley's work in a Latin American city argues that market place trading has continued to flourish in most cities and notes that dynamism in market place trading is associated with government intervention, with principal policies being the creation of markets outside traditional trading sites in the centre (Bromley, 1998). The social importance of markets has thus received minimal attention, notwithstanding some recent work on social interaction and conflict in a north London market (Watson and Wells, 2005; Wells and Watson, 2005).

## Policy and practice relevance

Markets are key sites of public space for many localities, and potentially offer opportunities not only for local economic development and employment, but also for social interaction and connection, social inclusion, the mingling of different cultures and the building of a sense of local community. There is a growing interest in the use of markets as focal points for local regeneration and community initiatives, but little is known as to why some markets succeed – economically and socially – and others do not. This study set out to consider some of these issues.

## Aims

This project aimed to:

1. Investigate the extent to which markets operate as social spaces for different groups in the community – as defined by socioeconomic group, age, gender, race and ethnicity.
2. Explore the different ways in which different groups use the space of the market (a) as stall holders and (b) as consumers.
3. Investigate how inclusive or exclusive the market is of different groups (a) as stall holders and (b) as users/consumers.
4. Explore levels of engagement and interaction between different individuals and groups in the market.
5. Assess the success of the market as a vibrant social, economic and cultural space for the city/town/borough in which it is located.
6. Provide a number of conclusions for local authorities on good practice and policy for local markets.

## Methods

Eight markets were selected for the research to reflect a range of different socioeconomic and cultural population profiles and also types of market. Two were in country towns, one partially covered and attached to a shopping centre (Lowestoft) and one in the open air (Ludlow). Three were in medium-sized to large northern cities, where one was entirely covered and enclosed in a shopping centre (St Helens) and two comprised indoor and outdoor markets (Preston, Rotherham). One was an outdoor market adjacent to a shopping centre in the Midlands (Milton Keynes), another was an outdoor street market (Ridley Road) in London, and the last was a farmer's market also in London (Islington). Following pilot visits to each site, every market was visited on between four and six occasions for all the days that it operated; there were several other visits of shorter duration, and visits were made at different times during the year to take account of seasonal variation.

Four methods of data collection were employed:

1. **Detailed observation of social interaction in the market was carried out and recorded at focal points in the market site** – for example, the café, the entrance, a food van – on each of the visits. Information recorded included gender, age, ethnicity[1] of individuals engaged in social interaction, form of social interaction – greetings, chats between shoppers, trader-shopper relationships, place and length of interaction, conflicts and tensions – and any other relevant information.

2. **Interviews were conducted with shoppers, traders and local officials**, all of which were recorded and transcribed. Most of these were one-to-one interviews. Traders' interviews were held during trading hours – because traders were keen to leave at the end of the day – and were therefore often interrupted. Typically, interviews ranged from 15 to 30 minutes, although some were longer. In each market, between 10 and 20 interviews with traders were conducted. Efforts were made to interview across a range of stalls, and to include the chair of traders in each market. Shoppers were approached and interviewed within the market site and in cafés in, or adjacent to, the market (these were more productive). Shoppers' interviews tended to be harder to secure and shorter – from five to15 minutes, with some exceptions. Efforts were made to interview a variety of shoppers in terms of gender, age and – where possible – ethnicity. Some shoppers, particularly Asian (and possibly Muslim),

---

[1] Age was considered in terms of age bands. Ethnicity was only tentatively noted.

appeared suspicious of the interviewers. In the current sociopolitical climate in Britain, this response was perhaps not surprising. The majority were interviewed individually, although a significant minority (one third) were interviewed in pairs or groups. Between 20 and 40 shoppers were interviewed in each locality. Market managers and local authority officials with direct responsibility for the market, and other relevant local officers – in, for example, tourism and regeneration departments – were also interviewed in each locality (from five to10 in each site).

3. **Photographs of each market** were taken during the research visits to capture how people were using the markets and to show key features of the sites.

4. **In-depth interviews (seven, each lasting one to two hours) were conducted with the following national informants**: the managers of Manchester Market, Borough Market and Leicester Market; the chair of NABMA; staff from the National Federation of Market Traders (with whom a focus group was held); a representative of the Towns Centre Initiative; and an official from the London Farmers' Association.

The interview material was thematically coded and analysed, and three key themes and several sub-themes emerged as significant to the running of a market and its social interaction. These were the locations and physical/spatial aspects of markets; the economic and product aspects of markets; and the management of, and strategies for, markets. Social interaction, customer profile, atmosphere, and conflict and tension were four further themes. These issues will be explored in Chapter 3 with the objective of considering the extent to which these more visible and recordable attributes of markets influence the success of markets as spaces of social interaction and vibrancy.

# 2

# The research sites

In order to explore the social role of markets, and the impact of different physical, economic and management factors on markets as spaces of diversity and social interaction, markets in six British towns and cities, and two further sites in London, were selected for ethnographic study. The localities were chosen to reflect potential differences between markets in rural areas, small towns, cities and the metropolis, and between different types of market. The sites also varied across socioeconomic and social/ demographic indicators. A farmers' market, which is defined as a market selling only fresh locally grown produce, was also studied to explore this relatively new market form as social space. This chapter gives a brief description of each market, drawing on 2001 census data from the Office of National Statistics, the Department for Communities and Local Government's 2001 Indices of Deprivation and local information sources.

Ludlow market

*Photo: David Studdert*

South Shropshire has a population of 40,410. The vast majority of the population is white (99.1%). The town is a popular retirement destination, with 26% of the population over retirement age and only 3% of households forming lone-parent families. This is a relatively wealthy population with a very high proportion of outright owner occupiers – 43.5% compared with 29% nationally, and 28.5% owners with a mortgage. The deprivation index is 206 (where 1 represents the most deprived locality and 354 the least deprived locality in England). Ludlow is a small medieval market town, with predominantly Georgian architecture, set in a pretty rural area. It is known as a 'foody' town and is popular with tourists who visit the castle, tea shops, craft shops and cultural facilities.

The council-run market is open five days a week, including Saturdays, in the town square at the top of the town. There are 43 erected sites and four extra vans on Saturdays. There are also a number of specialist markets that run periodically, including the May fair, the food and drink market in September, and the flea market. The old covered market was knocked down over 20 years ago, and resituated in a large open square near the castle, much to many locals' dismay because people appreciated the facilities and protection from weather provided by the old market. There are a range of stalls at the weekday market, including fruit and vegetables, flowers and cheese stalls run for many years by local families, as well as clothes and general household goods stalls. In addition, more specialised product stalls sell picture frames, teas, crafts, Indian jewellery, Russian coffee machines and other products. Although these stalls are patronised by locals, they are more oriented to the tourist trade. There is a tea van on the market site, but no café, although there are many tea shops close by. Local parking is fairly restricted,  although there is a small council parking area within walking distance. Of all the sites surveyed, Ludlow has the poorest transport linkage.

Photo: Sophie Watson

Ridley Road market

Ridley Road market is located in the east London borough of Hackney, which has a population of 202,824. This is a very ethnically and racially diverse area: 59.4% of the population is White, 8.6% Asian British and 24.7% Black African or African-Caribbean British. There is a relatively young population (average age 33), and a high proportion of lone-parent families (10%). The borough is one of the poorest councils in England – the deprivation index is 5, only 10% of households are outright home owners, 20.6% are owners with a mortgage and 50.6% are either local authority or housing association tenants.

The council-run market is situated on a relatively narrow street off Kingsland High Road and open every day of the week (except Sunday). The market has been in existence for more than a century (the exact date of its opening is hard to ascertain), and from the early 20th century was dominated by Jewish traders. The ethnic/racial diversity of the market, both in its shoppers and traders, is now extremely marked. In terms of traders, the market includes Africans, African-Caribbeans, Asians and Eastern Europeans, as well as retaining Jewish families who have traded at the market for many years and who continue to occupy the key fruit and vegetable and household goods stalls at the most visible end of the market. Every imaginable fruit and vegetable, along with ethnic food products and household goods, are sold on the stalls and, in the small shops, with hand-painted signs, anything from African hair pieces to meat and fish, loans and travel is available, making the site a vibrant multi-ethnic area. There is limited meter street parking nearby. The market is adjacent to a large mall, which includes Sainsbury's supermarket, where there is further parking. There are several food vans in the market and two small cafés hidden away.

Rotherham market

*Photo: David Studdert*

Rotherham is an old de-industrialised town of 248,175 people where the population is 96.9 % White, with an Asian community of 2.2 %. The council has a deprivation index of 63. Its loss of jobs in the coal and steel industries has left a population that is seriously affected by unemployment, particularly among the young. Twenty-three per cent of households are local authority tenants, compared with 13% nationally, and 26% are owner occupiers. Poverty and ill health are concerns, and there is a relatively high proportion of 16- to 74-year-olds with no qualifications (36.9%).

Rotherham's market includes an indoor council-run market of 88 stalls, which runs from Monday to Saturday, and an outdoor – recently renovated and partially covered – market of 131 stalls, which runs on Tuesday, Friday and Sunday. There is also a bric-a-brac market on Wednesday. The inside market has two levels. On the second level, stalls include lighting, electrical goods, clothes, delicatessen foods, books, household goods, makeup, bakery, handbags and luggage. In the same complex, there is a café, a number of advice and community centres, and a women's centre. In the downstairs inside market, there is a large variety of stalls and many places to sit down. The market is in the centre of the town, close to the station, and five minutes' walk from a large car park.

Photo: David Studdert

St Mary's Market, St Helens

St Helens is a city of 176,843 people, of whom 99% are White. Pilkington's Glass was formerly a key employer in the town, but its role has declined as the industry has become increasingly mechanised, with a resulting high unemployment rate in the town. The deprivation index in St Helens is 36. A significant 35.3% of people of employment age have no qualifications. Nineteen per cent of households are local authority tenants, 30% outright owner occupiers. There is a relatively large proportion of single-parent households (8%).

The council-run St Mary's indoor market is open Monday to Saturday. There are 90 stalls, many of which are not occupied. The range of products is limited to cheap clothes, accessories, make-up, mobile phones and other cheap household products. There are no food stalls except for a pork butcher. There is one café in the centre of the market site. The market has been recently relocated as a result of council-led redevelopment. Although the new building is bright and well designed, the front of the market faces a street that is rarely used and all the stalls at the front are empty– with fake painted stalls painted on the closed shutters giving the entrance a surreal feel. The café in the centre also acts to cut off, rather than integrate, one side of the market from the other. The other side of the market adjoins a busy but dilapidated shopping mall through a small entrance that is easy to miss. There is parking nearby in a multi-storey car park, and the bus station is a five-minute walk away.

Lowestoft has a population of 112,342. The population is almost exclusively White (98.8%). The deprivation index is 113, placing the council in the top third of deprivation ratings. One quarter of households are over retirement age. A significant 35.8% of 16- to 74-year-olds have no qualifications (compared with 29% nationally), and there are a highly visible number of people with disabilities, mental and physical, living in the town.

The council-run market is situated in the centre of town behind a large shopping centre – the Britten Centre – in the main high street. The main entrance from the street is through

Lowestoft market

the Centre. The market occupies a small space, which is adjacent to the public library and a café with outside seats and tables. There is an entrance to the bus station, and another to the town centre car park. The market is open for five days, including Saturday. There are three rows of permanent market stalls, which are partially protected from the weather – 36 stalls in total – selling a good range of products with many different products on different days (such as baby clothes, fish, picture frames), as well as stalls that are present every day when the market is open, including fruit and vegetables, sweets and a make-up stall. The market has recently been refurbished with a grant from the Sunshine Coast Regeneration Fund, and the stalls are all covered with brightly painted shutters that are locked up at night.

Milton Keynes is a post-war new town 60 miles north of London with a population of 207,057. It has a relatively low level of deprivation – 204 on the index – and good employment levels. Ten per cent of the population are Black or Asian British. There is a relatively young population with an average of age of 35.2 and levels of qualifications are comparatively high (under a quarter have no qualifications). There is also a relatively high percentage of householders with a mortgage – 47% compared with 38% nationally.

The market is run by a private company – Bray and Associates – every day of the week including weekends. The market is outside, with no protection from the weather, and is located at the centre of the city (which is spread across a wide area in a multi-centred form), adjacent to a large shopping centre, at some distance from the bus and train stations but close to bus stops and parking. It is partially under a flyover, which gives the site a rather depressing feel. The market has a very wide range of products, from fruit and vegetables to light furniture and household accessories. There is no café in the market – although there is a food and tea van – but there are cafés close by in the shopping centre.

Photo: Sophie Watson

Milton Keynes market

Preston is a town of 129,630 people with a comparatively large Asian British population (11.6%). The deprivation index is 59. The average age is low – 30, compared with 38.6 nationally. Twenty-six per cent of households are outright home owners (compared with 29.5% nationally); there is a high proportion of householders who are housing association tenants (21.6%), compared with 6% nationally, and a much lower proportion of local authority tenants (6.8 %) than the national figure (13.2%).

Preston has a council-run indoor market, open Monday to Saturday. On the ground floor, 75 stalls sell fresh produce – fruit, vegetables, bread and traditional Lancashire food such as black pudding, as well as a very wide range of household goods, clothing (including Goth) and miscellaneous products. Upstairs, there are 60 stalls, which also sell a wide range of non-food items from jewellery and haberdashery to sportswear and children's clothes. There is a café located on this floor. Next to the market hall under a Victorian canopy, there is a four-day-a-week outdoor market with a wide variety of goods. On Thursdays, this site is transformed into a large car-boot sale/flea market with 160 stalls. The initial impression is of easily accessible parking and a well-signposted market. The car park, however, is grimy and more expensive than at the other sites. Across the road, there is a smaller covered area adorned with the same Victorian ironwork and design. Here, the stalls are more scattered and there are obvious empty spaces.

Islington is a London borough with a high level of deprivation overall, reaching deprivation 6 on the index. One quarter of the population is non white, 5.4% are Asian British and 11.9 % Black African or African-Caribbean British. There is a relatively young demographic (average age 34.7). There are low proportions of outright owners (10%) and owners with a mortgage (21.1%), with 35.6% of householders living as local authority tenants. However, in the immediate vicinity of the market, there is considerable wealth following 20 years of gentrification of the local housing stock.

*Photo: David Studdert*

Preston market

Islington farmers' market is run by London Farmers' Markets (LFM) – an independent company managing 13 farmers' markets. These are markets in which farmers and producers from an area within 100 miles of the M25 set up their own stalls to sell their own produce direct to the market. LFM seeks out new sites for markets, and supports and encourages local community involvement in their establishment and ongoing activity, as well as promoting and running the markets once established. Each stall pays rent to LFM to subsidise these activities. The markets are located in a variety of sites, including station car parks, school playgrounds and public spaces in the middle of private developments. Islington is London's first farmers' market. At the beginning of the research, the market was located in Camden Passage – a row of antique and other shops opposite Islington Green and next to Tesco's supermarket. Over the years, as a result of its success, the market stalls and customers were overflowing out of their allocated space, making it difficult for people to move. In September 2005, therefore, it was relocated to a primary school playground at William Tyndale School. The current site is rather hidden off a main high street. Parking on Sunday here presents few problems and the local tube and train station is 10 minutes' walk away, with buses running close by. There is a wide range of fresh and organic produce. There is no café in the market, although there is food to eat, including lamb burgers cooked on site.

## Conclusion

It should be clear from this chapter that markets do not form a single entity; on the contrary, they are very heterogeneous, offering different provision and playing contrasting roles in different localities. The markets in this study were selected to explore some of these variations. Ridley Road is unique as the only street market in the study. Located as it is in a poor and highly racially diverse area, it plays a significant role in providing a very wide variety – in ethnic terms – of low-cost fruit, vegetables, meat, fish and other food items, which meet the diverse needs of the local community. St Helens market is the only entirely indoor market integrated into a low-cost shopping centre. It largely comprises cheap clothes and goods, which compete with the low-cost items to be

Photo: Sophie Watson

Islington farmers' market

found in the shopping centre. Ludlow represents the classic traditional market town model and, in providing a diversity of good-quality fresh food and a wide range of goods, serves the long-established local community as well as tourists in the town. Rotherham and Preston markets are similar in that they combine indoor and outdoor markets and provide a very good range of fresh food, household goods and clothes, which match well the needs of a predominantly white working-class local community. Lowestoft market, which is small with good-quality food and other products, is part of the local shopping centre and high street, thus providing one shopping opportunity among many for this relatively low-income and older white community. Milton Keynes is a large outdoor market attached to a shopping centre and with a more visible and separate presence. This market sells a diversity of goods, fresh fruit and vegetables, and other food items, but appears to appeal more to the low-income households in the local ethnically mixed community than the more professional and higher-income groups that also live locally. Islington was differentiated by its status as a farmers' market, providing fairly expensive high-quality fresh and organic produce to a predominantly middle-class and white local community.

This diversity of markets and the communities they serve raises important questions as to the different social roles that markets can play in different localities. These will be considered in the next chapter of this report.

# 3

# Markets as sites for social interaction

Markets clearly operate as key sites of sociability, but the form that this takes and the different people involved vary across different market sites, conditions and locations. Markets were found to provide four different social functions through this research – specifically, through the opportunities they provided for social interaction, the formation of social ties, social mixing across groups and social inclusion. Social interaction can range from a very minimal connection, such as a greeting between acquaintances or between shoppers and traders, to extended conversations between those who have met up in the market, or extended interactions between stallholders and the customers they serve. This engagement can lead to the formation of weak social ties, but markets can also serve as sites of stronger social bonding where friends and families trade together and form a particular community, or where traders and regular shoppers get to know each other over time. Social mixing refers more specifically to interactions across different socioeconomic, demographic and ethnic/racial groups. Finally, a market's role as a site of social inclusion refers to the fact that it can operate well as a public space where marginalised groups come to spend time, thereby providing opportunities to escape isolation in the home or elsewhere, while also providing an economically inclusive space – for example, by offering cheap goods that may not be available elsewhere.

This chapter explores some of the ways in which the social life of markets became clear in the research. These fall into five categories: the social life of traders; shoppers' and traders' relationships; markets as social spaces for different groups of shoppers; ethnic/racial differences and social relations in market sites; and conflicts and tensions in market social relations. The chapter concludes with some reflections on the different kinds of social role the markets served across the sites.

## Social life of traders

Although the importance of social relations between traders may not at first glance seem a crucial aspect of markets as spaces of social interaction, the reality is otherwise. For many traders, being a stallholder in a market constitutes a key aspect of their own social life:

> 'Everyone gets to know each other because you're standing there all day. Especially when it's dead quiet and you have to talk to the person next to you.'
> (Ludlow, trader)

> 'They always want to be in the same place, they don't want to move. And they tend to sort of form nice relationships with those that they're next to fortunately.'
> (Islington, manager)

Employment and social life for these people is thus inextricably linked. Where there is a diverse racial and ethnic composition of traders, as is particularly remarkable in Ridley

Road market, for example, market trade provides a key site for the meeting and management of differences across cultures in the local community. For example, the long-established Jewish traders spoke of helping the new Asian traders settle into the market, explaining the customs and practices of market life.

The interviews with both shoppers and traders revealed that the social atmosphere and vibrancy of a market were greatly enhanced in markets where traders had strong connections between themselves. This could take various forms. The majority of markets have traders' associations, which negotiate with market managers and councils. Where these are strong, with an articulate chair, the changing needs of the market are more likely to be addressed and improvements initiated. In many markets, traders give considerable practical support to one another, minding the stall in the owner's absence, helping to carry things and so on: 'If anyone's in trouble, everyone will always help you out, you know it's…. Well if you need fixtures, fittings, you know it's like if your car breaks down, you need a hand…. Yeah everyone's always ready to help, you know' (Milton Keynes, trader).

In some instances, it is evident that social interaction can lead to the formation of weak social links between people, which have the potential to develop into stronger bonds as people get to know each other.

Traditionally, market stalls were passed down between parents and children, often over many generations. And in many markets, families of siblings and cousins would own a number of stalls, often in proximity to one another. In Ludlow, for example, the cheese stall, owned by one trader, is opposite the flowers and vegetables, which are owned by his parents-in-law, who have been at the market for 50 years. In Ridley Road, the chair of traders comes from a Jewish family, which over generations has run the majority of stalls at the top of the market:

> 'Going back, it was all family-run markets, so there was loads of family and friends that ran the markets. There was about 70 families here … you had the Caines, the Moseleys, the Greys, the Lamberts … it had a nice social side to it…. It was very, very Jewish…. But then, Jewish people couldn't work on a Saturday. So some of the Jewish traders would give up their pitch to someone else on a Saturday. But then, times change, and the Jewish people started to move away … and we got loads and loads of Greeks, Cypriots, Turkish people. That was another good era we had.'

Still today, this respondent's cousins own five of the stalls, including the egg stall, where the owner's father was the publican at the main local pub, the Ridley Arms. These strong family connections provide a sense of social cohesion and often exuberant banter between the stalls, creating a vibrant social atmosphere. This pattern of family relationships was also found in Ludlow, and to a lesser extent other markets, although several people, including the longest serving trader at Rotherham, reported a dwindling of this practice as children who, traditionally, had followed their parents into the market, sought other jobs. Whether or not traders are related, the background sound of chatter and banter between traders who are acquainted creates a particular atmosphere in a market.

## Shoppers' and traders' relationships

Given that traders represent the visible centre of the market community, how they conduct themselves strongly affects the way a market feels to those who visit. As the chair of the traders at Ridley Road put it:

'If it's a bubbly, buzzy place and the traders are bubbly and buzzy, then obviously you get customers feeling comfortable.... In this day and age there is a hell of a lot more personal stress ... the council put a lot more pressure on certain traders than they have to and it reflects on the customers in the market.'

A striking theme that emerged from the interviews with shoppers was the importance of their relationships with the traders, which is markedly different from the experience of shopping in supermarkets:

'Oh, I'd talk to them, you know, chit-chat. But also about advice on particular things, like if I hadn't cooked something before I'll talk to them about how you cook it and they're always very helpful with that. And yeah I ask them how it's going, because I'm very conscious that it's pretty hard work for them, I can't imagine how they make a living. So I partly want to make them feel good, and I want to make myself feel good by feeling like I'm connecting with people.' (Islington, female shopper, late forties)

'They're more personal, personable, and you know some people when you talk to them about their produce, or their products, they're very excited about it, because they've really put a lot of effort into it. You go to the lady who sells honey and she's really into bees and she talks a lot about how to look after the bees, and you know she's really excited.' (Islington, black male, late forties)

For many shoppers, the daily or weekly interaction they had with traders was cited as a key reason for going to the market, even if they reported no other social exchange on the market site. Many reported the pleasure of banter as a form of social interaction with market traders. In some markets, traders performed an exaggerated theatricality that appeared to contribute to their stalls' success as well as enhancing the shoppers' experience. A notable example here was the woman sheep farmer from Battle who sold lamb and homemade lamb-burgers at the Islington farmers' market and took pleasure in teasing and being rude to her customers, who reported being amused too.

Simon Quin from the Town Centres Initiative highlighted the importance of theatre as an attraction in markets, but noted how diversity in offer could add to this:

'I think markets should be about theatre and the continental markets are a theatre just because they're foreign in effect, but some of the traditional markets have that as well. I think interestingly some of that theatre can come through – you know we're talking continental markets but actually many of our ethnic markets, traditional markets that have become ethnic markets, have really become as foreign as the continental markets ... they're actually forming a tourist attraction, they benefit tourists, in inverted commas, or are an attraction for the general population.'

However, a St Helens trader regretted that:

'We are not allowed to pitch in the market in the mall. But I do it at the outdoor markets. I like to shout at the girls. So I do pitch. Pitching definitely creates a market atmosphere. There are certain councils and boroughs around the country that allow it. Bolton market is one, so is Leeds. But it can frighten people, especially the elderly.'

Many traders in all markets also commented on the relationships they had with regular customers:

'You do notice more on a Tuesday when it is more older people. You know they tend to have a good look round, want to have a chat with you. And you do see the same faces; more or less the same times each day, each week.' (Milton Keynes, trader)

'I have a lot of regulars. I've got a lot of my ladies who are very regular on their ribbons and they do a lot of knitting. Not just for their own children or grandchildren, they knit for charities or for like one of the hospitals, like the premature baby unit. It's very hard to buy premature babywear, so they do all their knitting. They do all the tiny mittens and bonnets and everything and they go through yards and yards of – or, I must be correct, metres and metres of ribbon.... I mean they don't know me by name. They can pass me in the street and go, "Oh that's my button lady" or "That's my ribbon lady", you know, things like that. And that's really nice. They chat and say, "Have you got anything new in" or "Can you get so and so".' (Lowestoft, trader)

'I get on with my customers and I make them feel special ... they actually say, "Mick, sort me out, get me an outfit" ... they feel comfortable with me because I can say, there you go, bang, bang, bang, that's yours ... right, next! I'd say about 90% of my customers know me by name. That's the kind of relationship I have with them.' (Preston, trader)

'If you're relying on people to come into the market in the rain, then the core customers are, you know, your mainstay really.' (Ludlow, trader)

Long-term traders who worked more often – commonly the fruit and vegetable and other food traders (as opposed to stallholders who worked markets on a one-day-a-week basis) – frequently referred to the loyalty of their shoppers, and the way in which they kept an eye on long-term customers. In this capacity, they acted as focal points for the community for passing information about a local person's health or state of their marriage.

## Markets as social spaces for different groups of shoppers

Markets perform different roles for different social groups, and their importance and use among the population can vary according to age, gender and other factors. This research considers the role that markets play for older people, families with children, young people and people with disabilities.Older people

The single most striking finding about who uses markets as social spaces is how crucial they are in the daily life of older people – more than for any other group:

'We've missed a generation. The young generation aren't using the market. They go down to Next and whatever. And a lot of our customers are the elderly. They still come faithfully to Preston market, come rain or shine. They'll be here every Friday morning at nine o'clock, come what may. And when they die, nobody is going to replace them. But that type of person is now literally on their last legs.' (Preston Council, official)

The market is also predominantly a social space for older women rather than older men. This is not to say that in many instances other groups cannot be found shopping in markets; rather, it is to emphasise the social importance of markets for this group. This was true of all markets with the possible exceptions of Ridley Road and Islington farmers' markets, which appealed to a wider diversity of social groups as a place to linger and

*Photo: David Studdert*

Ludlow market

chat. In the markets that had cafés on site, like St Helens and Rotherham, older people typically sat down in the café for tea or a meal for an hour, and often longer, with partners, friends and family. Sometimes this was with people with whom they had come, and sometimes with those they had 'bumped into' in the market. In St Helens, where the majority of stalls in the market were reporting difficulties, the café at the centre was full throughout the day with older people sometimes chatting for hours. The fact that the café occupied a key central location meant it offered views across the entire site and enough activity to create interest for the people sitting there without the more frantic atmosphere of the shopping centre. It was also an attraction for older people being taken on an outing by carers. One trader in St Helens reported:

> 'A lot of elderly people use this market. Because they are a bit more frail or
> fragile or frightened, they find the "multinational" too busy, too rushed. Because
> this market is quieter, they can feel more at ease. But the market caters for every
> age. For example, X over there is selling teenage tops.' (St Helens, trader)

In markets where there was no café immediately on site, such as Ludlow and Lowestoft, older people typically repaired to cafés or tearooms nearby, while in Milton Keynes and Lowestoft, where the market was adjacent to a shopping centre, a common pattern was for the older people who had shopped in the market to return to the warmth and comfort of the shopping centre. Many of them would then sit for long periods of time on circular benches around flower beds or in the other formal seating areas provided there. The greeting of acquaintances and friends, and stopping to chat, was frequently observed.

Formal seating, such as the benches provided in the indoor market at Preston, and informal seating, often barely visible in markets, also appeared to represent significant sites of social interaction for older people. They both needed to sit down to rest and also appeared to enjoy the informality and lack of expense associated with this activity. Not all of them could afford to spend money in cafés. As one woman in Rotherham said, 'Only posh people go to coffee shops'. This comment reflects the important role of some markets in providing a socially inclusive space for people on lower incomes.

Café, St Mary's Market, St Helens

An interesting aspect of the informal seating arrangements in Rotherham was their gendered nature. The majority occupying 'the form' on the upstairs balcony were men, while downstairs, on the blue seats in the 'smoking corner', women in their sixties and seventies gossiped with others who shared the space on a regular basis. They said they knew each others' faces but not necessarily their names.

The physical attributes of a market had a strong impact on its use as a social space for older people. The importance of seating has already been highlighted. Transport was the other key issue for older people in all market sites. Carrying heavy bags over even short distances was cited as an inhibiting factor, which militated against older people using markets. Given that this group tends to have lower car ownership or usage, bus stops adjacent to markets appeared to be crucial.

As the market manager at St Helens said:

'I'm not physically going to be able to change the market. But I think in order to revitalise the market it is important to get back to basics. Markets are traditionally for people on lower incomes. They tend to use buses or public transport to get here. It's no good having a market where you've got fruit and vegetable and the bus station's a mile and a half away. My idea was to build a mini bus station in front of the multi-storey car park. I've got to bring people in, rather than hope people will try and find me.' (St Helens, market manager)

Despite the relative proximity of the bus station to this site, the manager's comments reflected problems in terms of the market's appeal, and disappointment in the market's relocation out of the centre.

In order to create a space for social contact, markets also need to provide a purpose for people to visit. The interconnection between the market and other amenities, in particular all-purpose shops, health centres, public libraries, post offices and community facilities, are key here, both for older people and for other visitors. In Preston, for example, the post office in the market had recently been closed down, which, according to the majority of traders, had led to a decline of visits to the market, particularly among older people. In Ludlow, Kwik Save supermarket, where many pensioners bought a few household goods during their visit to the market, had also recently closed, with reported detrimental effects on the life of the market.

Other spatial and physical attributes of markets have a further impact on their use as social spaces by older people. The ease of moving between stalls and the width of aisles, for example, are two such considerations. Shoppers in Ridley Road would need to be strong enough to withstand jostling, and a wheelchair there would be harder to manage than in Lowestoft, Preston or Ludlow. The lack of easy access to toilet facilities was a concern for all groups, but older people in particular frequently cited it as a problem.

Finally, traders claimed to play a strong role in keeping an eye on older people – for example, in Rotherham, a long-established trader, whose stall was located close to the 'form' where the older people (mainly men) sat, described how her 92-year-old father (also formerly a market trader) had only recently stopped spending time there every day, and how she always offered older people tea and water, and attended to their needs. 'All the traders do the same', she said.

## Families with children

During weekdays, the second most visible group of users of markets as social spaces was women with pre-school children. This group, like older visitors, also typically used the cafés provided on market sites. Respondents in this group were difficult to interview because they were usually preoccupied with childcare activities. Rather than the market functioning as a site of casual encounter, typically these younger women came with their mothers or with friends who also had young children. Shopping for this group appeared to be a more functional activity, particularly among poorer women searching for cheaper commodities. Neither the women themselves nor the traders in any of the markets commented on the shopper–trader relationship as being very significant to them. But there were exceptions. The woman in charge of the make-up stall in St Helens market frequently kept an eye on the children while their mothers, who regularly patronised her stall, ducked across the aisle to Girl Talk, which was one of the few successful stalls in the market.

In all the markets in the study, on Saturdays (and on Sundays in Islington farmers' market) families with children represented the major group of shoppers. Unlike the previous group, many of these families saw the markets as sites for various forms of social interaction or interest for the children. As one woman said: 'If you have children, it is better being here than at Tesco's. Things are lower down, there is always something going on, something for them to look at (Ludlow, female shopper)'.

And another shopper in Ludlow commented:

'My kids hate going to the shops but they like going to the market … particularly the boys. I don't know whether it's claustrophobia or what, but the market they love…. They say they like the outside and it's just more of an exciting environment I think. There's lots of different stalls.' (female shopper)

Time spent on market visits tended to be longer at the weekend, because children commonly bumped into friends from school, and parents also bumped into acquaintances from the locality and then stopped to chat. The manager of Islington farmers' market put it this way:

'I think they knew each other already but then they meet friends of friends or they bring their grown up daughter or their grown up daughter brings their mum from the country – that kind of thing. So it is very sociable, I have to keep saying 'excuse me, I can't get past', because they're all stopping, chatting in the aisle and they have interesting conversations.'

*Photo: Sophie Watson*

Islington farmers' market

The London farmers' markets coordinator also described another site as an important place for families:

'Wimbledon Park is in a school yard. This is another one of our farmers' markets in Wimbledon, in a nice little residential area, so all our customers are very local and they all come every Saturday morning with their bags ready. They all know each other and their kids went to the school.'

In this site, the market visit was greatly enhanced by the presence of play equipment, as the coordinator noted

'There's climbing equipment and play equipment for kids, so quite often parents and families will spend a bit of time there as well and, you know, use it as a sort of a morning out for the children. Similarly, at Queens Park that's also happening as well ... and, and to some extent Marylebone as well.... If you spend any time at a market, you will see the same people over the course of an hour, and they might well do a bit of shopping at the market, go off for a coffee and then come back and do a little bit more or finish off and get something they forgot to buy.'

This feature had been identified as a stimulus for activity in St Helens, where one of the market assistant's ideas to address the empty space in the market was to place play equipment there.

As mentioned earlier, a market visit is frequently punctuated by a visit to a local café or casual eating at a food stall or caravan. Islington farmers' market, like other farmers' markets, was striking in this respect. The quality and range of products sold, and the fact that traders offered samples for shoppers to try, meant that groups formed around the stalls, and strangers and acquaintances would frequently chat for quite lengthy periods of time. The opportunity to sample new foods and drinks was particularly attractive to children, who could be seen to grab more than once piece at a time. In all the markets, food vans were well used by parents and their children, who tired of shopping without sustenance.

### Adults without, or not accompanied by, children

Many people visit markets alone, across the whole age range, and in all markets women outnumbered men. For many of the group discussed here (adults aged from their late twenties to late fifties), markets were seen as a site of social interaction. These were typical comments from the shoppers and the manager at Islington farmer's market:

'I think the public do go to the pub afterwards sometimes or they go for a coffee together or something. I hear people saying, "Well let's meet at such and such after you've been to the book shop" or you hear all these things. "When will you be round for lunch?" And I'm always recommending where people can go 'cause we have this organic pub round the corner.' (Market manager)

'Yeah, I already have bumped into someone – a colleague – not a colleague, but somebody from my profession who I haven't seen for two years.' (Middle-aged woman)

'This is my wife, my partner's there. She comes – we always come, mostly come together, because we enjoy it – it's nice, you know, get up in the morning and you know it's fresh, Sunday morning and you come and you look around and you see people … and I like the fact that people are here with their kids and they're all outside and I love the smell of the burgers.' (Middle-aged man)

'I just think it's like a proper, it's the nearest thing to community at work, do you know what I mean?' (Female shopper)

'I think it's a real wonderful thing for a community, because you see the same people coming and it's so completely different from shopping in a supermarket.' (Female shopper)

'I would normally come on my own, but I've been with friends before, so if I've got friends staying with me, I bring them.' (Female shopper)

Younger and middle-aged adults were generally far less present in the markets than older people or people with children, with the exception of Islington farmers' market (which has a more middle-class clientèle) and Ridley Road. The latter market represented a significant social meeting place for many people of different cultures – African-Caribbean, African, Eastern European, Latin American and Chinese people, among others – because people of all ages, including many younger age groups, saw the market as a place where acquaintances and old friends could be found. Here, too, there was a notably different gender mix, with a large number of young and middle-aged men in the market.

Various explanations were given by the traders for the declining presence of this adult age group. First, it was reported that supermarkets with free parking and longer shopping hours were more attractive to those in the workforce who might be shopping on their way to and from work and were frequently in a hurry. Second, changing expectations around shopping such as the use of credit and debit cards – commonly not an option at market stalls – discouraged this group of people from shopping in markets: 'The young people are brought up now, they want to pay by card, and they want to buy all under one roof. And of course it's cash in the market ... and they are not interested really'(Lowestoft, trader).

Catalogue and internet shopping has also grown in significance as a shopping activity among this group, with its greater flexibility for those in work. Others reported that markets were perceived as a fuddy-duddy, outmoded activity of their parents' generation: 'The younger generation are out of market habits, aren't they? You know the market, the younger generation, to walk around the market doesn't appeal to them whereas the generation before it was part and parcel (Milton Keynes, trader).'

There were also exceptions, however: 'It's more friendly than a supermarket.... You get to know the stall holders as well and they know you. So you've got a more personal shopping.... And you often meet up with people that you haven't seen for a while, because you have been working' (Ludlow, female shopper, around 35).

Young people working as traders in markets is also common. In Rotherham and St Helens, there were a number of young Asian traders, particularly selling products that appeal to younger shoppers, such as mobile phones and football shirts, while in Islington farmers' market, the manager reported: 'Quite a lot of them employ young people to work for them, very interesting, all different nationalities, we had 26 nationalities one week'.

## Young people (teens to mid-twenties)

While young and middle-aged adults were less commonly seen than older people in the markets studied, younger people – those aged in their teens and early to mid-twenties – were also less regular users of markets. A dominant narrative among traders in all the markets was the decline in the use of markets by young people over the past 20 years:

'Contemporary young people have not been through the abject poverty of earlier generations, going to school with holes in their shoes, etc. The market means nothing to them except the possibility of getting something cheaper.' (St Helens, trader)

'Young ones don't come in very much ... I'll give you an example with my children. Although some of them have worked with me here when they were at school, as soon as they leave they don't want to come to this market.... They like supermarkets.' (African female café owner)

Despite this gloomy narrative, some traders reported that a new interest in organic food and fresh produce promoted by celebrity chef Jamie Oliver and others, alongside a culture that emphasises healthy eating habits, was putting markets, particularly farmers' markets, firmly back on the map. Certainly, younger age groups were highly visible at Islington farmers' market. According to the trader selling cheese at Ludlow:

'About 10 years ago, when supermarkets were coming on strong ... they started to brainwash the younger generation – the younger married people spend their money in supermarkets. But in the last two years you can see a trend back to the markets again … they have said, "I don't like that cheese" and they come back for some decent quality cheese again.'

And in Lowestoft, this trader, when asked who used the market, responded:

'Across the ages, across the board really. Lots of youngsters come in. They have their dogs, they come and get their pet food on a regular basis. And you've got the old ladies who've got their budgies and dogs.'

Young people, particularly teenagers and college students, were typically observed to visit markets in groups, often during their lunch hour on college days. Here, the social activity focused on hanging around particular stalls that matched their interests and needs. For example, in Lowestoft, the make-up and accessories stall had a constant group of young women standing chatting by the stall and comparing items.

In Rotherham, the Goth stall represented a key social site. This often presumes a good relation with the trader. At one point in St Helens, a (white) girl of about 17 in a group of friends referred to the Asian mobile phone trader as 'her fancy piece', whom she joked with and visited every day. Groups of boys were also found to cluster around mobile phone stalls.

In Ridley Road, the 'Rasta man' (self-proclaimed) soap stallholder reported: 'Oh yeah! Youngsters come down here. Normally they buy, like, trainers, T-shirts and things but they don't buy food. Some come in groups. I've seen in here the younger people they are not bad … compared to other markets we used to go to.'

Where the market was adjacent to a college, as in Rotherham and Ludlow, groups of students were seen to hang around the market eating takeaway food and chatting during

Lowestoft market, make-up and accessories stall

*Photo: Sophie Watson*

lunch hours or breaks. A female respondent (25 years old) in Ludlow reported: 'When I was at college here, six or seven years ago, this was my first port of call before I went into the college. A cup of tea and a bacon buttie. This was the centre of it because the college is just there.'

In towns where there are relatively few facilities for young people, the market can function as a key social site, where young people laugh and flirt with one another. Milton Keynes was notable in this respect.

## People with physical disabilities

In the markets in towns with a high deprivation index, St Helens and Rotherham, and in Lowestoft, where there is a concentration of people on benefits, a striking sight was the prevalence of shoppers in motorised wheelchairs. St Helens, Rotherham and Preston all have shopmobility schemes. Observation of this group of shoppers revealed long stays in the market. Often these shoppers appeared relatively isolated but appeared to be enjoying the activity going on around them. One middle-aged man interviewed said that he knew no-one there, but he liked sitting watching people go by. A man in a wheelchair interviewed in Ridley Road similarly enjoyed this experience. Others came accompanied by carers, friends or partners and also bumped into friends there. The 'form' seating area occupied by the pensioners in Rotherham also had a constant stream of visitors in wheelchairs. For these shoppers to engage in the market, the width of the aisle and the physical layout of the cafés were reported to be of crucial significance. The need for parking for disabled people near the market was also mentioned: 'There is a lot of disabled parking around here. It gets the disabled people right into the middle of the town, and that is good' (Preston, trader).

Several respondents, who were not necessarily disabled but who were unwell, reported enjoying a visit to the market, for example:

> 'I've been off work for a few months now and it's keeping me in contact with people. So I quite enjoy popping in as frequently as I do at the moment … it's nice to come for the bustle and to meet people that you haven't seen for a long time … it's been a really nice place to come, interact with people without it being too long.' (Ludlow, female shopper)

Overall, where markets were accessible to wheelchair users, they appeared to function well as places where this group could be included in the social life of the community.

## Ethnic/racial differences and social relations in market sites

The use of markets is highly local, with some exceptions. A survey of shoppers at Islington farmers' market, for example, found that 60% lived within a mile of the market. As a result, markets usually reflect the social demographics of the locality in which they are placed in terms of their users and the produce on offer. The ethnic composition of traders, however, is more varied in larger towns, but not in small market towns such as Ludlow.

In this study, Rotherham and Milton Keynes were the most ethnically diverse sites, apart from Ridley Road, where the majority of the local population are not white. In Rotherham, traders reported relatively untroubled relations between people of different ethnicities, although there were clearly some tensions. The market manager said: 'There have been quite a lot of asylum seekers in Rotherham, mostly Eastern Europeans. They

Rotherham market

Photo: David Studdert

tend to congregate and chat. Some of the people in the market find that quite intimidating.' One Asian woman, on seeing the interviewer, expressly elected to be interviewed, and reported observing such high levels of antagonistic attitudes from the fruit and vegetable traders towards herself and other Asian female shoppers that she refused to go to these stalls and sent her white husband to shop for her instead. This comment from a white woman shopper confirmed her point that some people's attitudes in the market were racist: 'How can I put it without being rude? They let coloured people play with the food ... the English people aren't allowed to touch it. So George won't go to that stall because he simply doesn't want his food mauled.'

In Milton Keynes, different ethnic/racial family groups appeared to keep themselves to themselves and mix little across communities, although in this location no inter-ethnic racial tension was reported. On the contrary, one Indian 45-year-old woman shopper said: 'To be honest, yeah, I've never seen, all the times I've ever been here, and I've been in Milton Keynes for years, I've never seen any hassle between people, never.'

In Preston, shoppers commented on the presence of Eastern Europeans:

Shopper 1 (Polish man, around 60): 'If you listen to people talking, you will hear a lot of different languages.'

Shopper 2: 'A hell of a lot of different languages.'

Shopper 1: 'Because a heck of a lot of Polish people come to Preston.'

Shopper 2: 'It's a big influx of East Europeans.'

Islington farmers' market, like other farmers' markets, attracted predominantly white customers. The site offer is clearly important in terms of how people use a site:

'What we found in Tower Hamlets was that the largely Bengali population were only interested in buying what they usually knew about and what they usually wanted which was specific vegetables and fruits that were imported from wherever, from Bangladesh. They were only interested in halal meat, for example, as well, which you know is kind of quite limiting if you've not got halal meat producers.' (London Farmers' Market officer)

Ridley Road, of all the market sites, according to traders and shoppers and from all observations, operated as perhaps the most vibrant social space for shoppers and traders between and across many different cultures. According to one trader:

'You get a lot of Jamaicans, Africans, Nigerians. They all live in the area. It's the old famous Ridley Road. This is like a meeting point for a lot of them. There are people down here who haven't seen each other for 20 years, and they have met in Ridley Road. You know, no other market but Ridley [is like that]. It must say something, you know.'

And the woman who runs the egg stall noted:

'There are lots of South American people down here now. Spanish, Brazilian, Cuban … there's a big community of South Americans coming up now. Chinese, you get a lot of Chinese people now. And Polish. Lots of Russians. Lots of different people shop here.'

The shoppers interviewed reported visiting the market regularly with the specific intention of bumping into acquaintances and long-lost friends, even to the extent of looking out for people last seen in their country of origin:

'Yeah, I do bump into people…. You meet people you have not seen for *years!*'

[Interviewer] 'Do you? From the local community?'

'From abroad! People from Nigeria come here, they are looking for me, they don't know my address…. I tell them everything because they have been looking for me for long. And eventually they found me here.' (Nigerian woman, late fifties)

Interestingly, the lack of formal seating areas did not deter vibrant social interaction here, and informal spaces, such as crates, empty stalls and steps of containers, were occupied throughout the day by many of the African and African-Caribbean communities, while groups of people were frequently seen standing by stalls:

'Yes, they'll collect in the street. If they see a friend or neighbours they'll just hang in there, stop, and start chatting. And in about 10 minutes they finish, it's up to them. Usually it doesn't trouble me. It happened to me once, I said, "Please can you move aside a bit for me", because they had been standing there for so long, chatting, chatting and blocking the stall.' (Soap stall trader)

'Sociable? Yeah! I come down here on a Saturday because I know if I'm going to bump into someone you can bump into them here on a Saturday. That used to be a big pub … and on a Saturday, I'll tell you what … they'd all be there and you could have a laugh and you used to meet your uncle there, your brother ….' (African-Caribbean woman, 37)

The closure of the long-established Ridley Arms pub in the middle of the market was mourned by many traders and shoppers as the loss of a crucial social space. But the role of the market here in bringing people together still seemed valuable. According to the traders, the market functioned not only as a space of social interaction but also social mixing. It facilitated the creation of social bonds across different ethnicities, particularly between the old Jewish families and more recent African-Caribbean and Asian traders. Some tensions, however, were reported. More negative feeling was attached to the more recent arrival of Eastern European traders and traders who did not share the English language.

## Conflicts and tensions in market sites

As the above comments on Ridley Road suggest, social tensions were occasionally evident. Respondents in a number of markets (particularly the poorer ones) in the study reported moments of tension and conflict, although, overall, market spaces appeared remarkably tension- and conflict-free. The most commonly cited issue was people using the space for taking drugs:

> 'There's a problem with drugs as in every market. We have found empty needles, that type of thing, syringes. The staff are trained to deal with this. The toilet tenants, team leaders, market tenants, all have radios. They have the direct numbers to the office. So if an incident happens, or there has been an accident, or shoplifting, they alert straight away.' (Rotherham, market manager)

Another issue cited was young people simply hanging about and being seen to create a nuisance for other shoppers:

> 'The same group of about six druggies has been in town for the last 10 years. From time to time they'll do something really bad and then they'll get caught and maybe put in prison. Then they are out and do the same thing again. We don't have much violence really with this particular group. Then you will get gangs of kids coming in … and because it's a gang of kids you think, oh, trouble! The majority don't cause any trouble but it can be a bit off-putting.' (St Helens, market assistant)

'Winos' were also cited as a problem in St Helens market, and bag snatching or stealing from stalls was reported as another source of tension. One trader in Preston told this story:

> 'We have a list of people who we know are really bad shoplifters. If they come up to you, you shoo them off quick…. What they do, though, is nick off one stall and then try and sell it to another stall. I had it done to me last week. Somebody pinched a game off my stall. They scammed me. And then they took it down to another stall and sold it there … I went mad at the other stallholder for buying it in the first place.'

Many of the markets had employed security guards with the result that the area was now seen as a safer social space. CCTV was also used on some sites:

> 'Every week somebody gets pickpocketed and people get scared. They've got a camera, but it's at the end of the market. They haven't got no camera in the middle.' (Rotherham, trader)

In Ridley Road, policing was more informal, which seemed to be a preferable approach:

Everybody knows me. I am the Rasta man who does soaps ... I am watching everybody and everybody is watching me. Everybody knows what everyone is doing. And if you are doing anything wrong, me personally, I do tell you straightaway.' (Soap stall trader)

## Conclusion

The research reported on in this chapter has revealed that markets operate as social spaces in a number of different ways for different social groups. This varied across the different sites, and also between different social groups. The social life of traders themselves played a significant role in helping to create a vibrant atmosphere in markets, at the same time as being of significance in forging links in that community itself. The interactions between traders and shoppers were also found to be a crucial component of the social life and interactions in the market, particularly for older people who regularly visit markets for the pleasure of these relationships. In these respects, the markets also functioned as sites of social bonding. Furthermore, they operated as sites of social inclusion, in the sense that for many of the customers, particularly those more marginalised in the city, passing the time of day in the market and chatting with a trader or another shopper might be the only chance they had to talk with someone all day. St Helens, and to a lesser extent Milton Keynes, appeared to offer fewer of these interactions, which were more common where there were longer established traders who had worked in the market for many years, and across generations. The exception to this pattern was Islington, where the market had no long-established pattern of use, but where the strong connection and involvement with their produce meant that traders were keen to engage with customers who shared their passion for fresh, locally grown food.

Markets were revealed to be sites of social interaction for all groups in the community, even younger people – despite a dominant narrative that this group had disappeared from market sites. However, there were differences between groups. Markets first and foremost represented a crucial place for social interaction in the lives of older people, and specifically older women, across all the sites. They were also seen as important social spaces for families with children, particularly on the weekends, when market shopping was a time to bump into friends, shop and chat at leisure. Young people enjoyed market visits in a different way from the former two groups, congregating around specific stalls and standing around chatting to friends.

Even where markets exhibit low levels of social interaction and/or the absence of some social groups in large numbers, if we see the social inclusion function of markets as a more limited form of social interaction, simply co-presence, the market's role as a place to stop and dwell for a while takes on greater significance. Given that markets also offer a wide range of affordable products to their customers, in this respect they also perform an important role in including low-income groups, who may be excluded from other shopping sites. The three groups for whom markets are most significant in this respect are older people, people with disabilities and young mothers, although, where there are problems of accessibility, the inclusiveness of markets for some groups may be constrained.

Finally, how did markets fare as sites of social mixing? Conflicts and tensions in markets were reported to be rare. However, there was some evidence of interracial tension at one of the sites, and some reports of shoplifting and drug use elsewhere, which had been tackled by an increase in security guards in some sites, and informal policing by the traders in others. Overall, the markets tended to reflect the sociodemographics of the local community and where this was very mixed, such as in Ridley Road, the market appeared to act as a site of mixing and connection in very positive ways. The markets as a whole, again with the exception of St Helens, also appeared to provide opportunities for some mixing across different age groups, particularly in café sites.

Overall, a significant number of shoppers in each site saw the market as a sociable space, even if they themselves did not go to the market specifically to meet friends or socialise. What is revealed here is the importance of exploring how different markets operate in different communities, drawing out the different social roles they may play. In other words, what works for one local community may not work for another. Policy agendas thus need to be sensitive to local needs and specificities. As this chapter has begun to show, some key attributes could contribute to markets' success as social spaces, including different economic, locational, physical and management factors. These are examined in the next chapter.

# 4

# The broader context

The focus of this chapter is on the extent to which markets' success as social spaces is affected by other factors. First, a market clearly cannot be viable if no one goes to shop there. Thus, the economic success of a market bears some relation to its success as a social space. Here, the notion of dwell time is important, because, if there is not much in a market, it is unlikely to keep its customers on site for long. As one trader in Preston put it: 'You need to have the people, you need to have the stalls, the influx of general public to come and look round the stalls. You know, without one, you can't have the other.' The strength of this relationship is not easy to quantify, but it clearly underpins the market's operation.

Second, if a market is in a poor location, badly designed, inaccessible by private or public transport, not protected from bad weather, and suffering from other negative physical attributes such as poor layout and design, these too are likely to have an impact on its success as a social space. The question to be addressed here is the extent to which these attributes matter for a market to be a site of social interaction, and, in particular, which factors are critical.

Third, there are a range of management or strategic elements that are likely to affect the economic and social success of a market, and this research considers how such factors can have an impact on its social life and vibrancy. The interviews revealed that these were issues that were important in varying degrees to both traders and shoppers.

This chapter considers the economic issues underpinning the operation of markets and the locational and physical attributes of the markets studied, as well as their management, in order to provide a context for understanding more fully how markets function as social spaces.

## The economic context

Given that, for the majority of people, the prime reason for visiting a market is to buy products, even if they also enjoy markets for social reasons, a diversity of traders and products will clearly also influence a market's success as a social space. Traders and shoppers in almost all the interviews commented on the importance of the quality of goods, their competitive prices and the range to be found in the market. Given steep competition from cheaper stores, this can be a serious issue:

> 'My wife buys the food on the local market in another town where we live. But she'll come back and say, why do I go and buy shirts in the market, or buy whatever for the kids, when I can go to Matalan? It doesn't cost me anything to park, I can take the article back if there's a problem with it, and there's no arguments … and it's quite a bit cheaper than the market. It's also centrally heated in winter. It's a hard one to answer.' (Preston Council, official)

Moreover, according to key informants – managers and traders – the success of a market depends on a good fit between the products and the local community. Kris Zasada (Manchester market) commented:

'Are the opening hours right for the community it's serving? Is the product mix right for the community it's serving? Is there a depth and range on offer, is there some sense of dynamism, some sense of change where there are new products and new traders coming in? Or is it the same faces that have been there for 25 years? If you've got a healthy mix and a dynamic mix, I think that is a strong indicator of a good, successful market.'

Farmers' markets, partly because the prices are higher, tend to attract a more middle-class section of the population. Thus, the farmers' markets were very popular in gentrified Islington and Ludlow, while attempts to introduce a farmers' market into Tower Hamlets in east London had been unsuccessful, according to the London Farmers' Market coordinator – in this case also because the Bengali population there wanted to buy halal meat or produce from their own country. Similarly, selling expensive goods in St Helens would not easily be viable, whereas in Ludlow:

'We're very lucky here, we have a very good variety of trades in the market. If you want a £5,000 diamond ring you can find it in the market, on a Saturday. If you want a circle ring, you could probably buy it today. We've got diamonds, we've got circle wedding rings. For good quality, we have two old fashioned antique ring stalls, where a lot of money is spent.' (Ludlow, trader)

A good variety and range of products seemed crucial to all markets as a minimum requirement for their success as social spaces. In Preston, there was a consistent view that the quality and range of goods in the market had declined in recent years, which was attributed to the uncertainty around the market's future and the fact that the market was held on too many days:

'At one time ... Preston market was the best in the North ... but now you're getting many one-type stalls. There's not a variety ... it's not a full market you know, there are lots of gaps ... at one time, on the outside market, you couldn't get a space. You had to wait for a pitch.' (Preston, trader)

'It's dying because there's not any variety. There's not enough specialised stalls. There's no different shoes – they are all the same. The clothes are all the same. There's about seven mobile phone stalls outside.' (Preston, trader)

Where key stalls are, or become, absent from a market, this can have a downward spiral effect, as occurred in the new St Helens market:

'The first three or four months were very good because people from outside the town were coming in to have a look at the new market and footfall was very good. Then we noticed that the odd stall was starting to struggle. The rents were a lot higher than anticipated and maybe trade wasn't as good. It was like a pack of cards. It happened in blocks. Somebody would leave which affected the guy next door so his trade dropped. Eventually he would go too, and then the next three or four blocks tended to go en masse. We lost the butchery department and the fish guy, which was a big blow. They are a big draw for any market.' (Chair of Stallholders Federation)

By contrast, in Ridley Road, which was one of the most vibrant of the markets in the study, the range and quality of fruit and vegetables and different ethnic foods was constantly referred to:

'See, a lot of people come here for the food. Especially if you're not from here, you know you can come to Ridley Road market and you can get your yam, your

dashi, your plantain. The Nigerians they can get their food ... the Chinese can get their food. But now, if you notice, there are more clothes stalls than food stalls.'
(Ridley Road, African-Caribbean woman shopper)

As such, the market draws many shoppers, particularly African and African-Caribbean, some from as far away as Birmingham and Kent.

The appearance and layout of a market plays a crucial role in attracting shoppers to the market and keeping them there, and hence in providing opportunities for social interaction. Anchor stalls, which pull people into the market, are therefore important, as is the attractive display of produce. Kris Zasada (Manchester market) notes:

'Strategic anchors are important and people really have to understand the importance of the retail profile of that market. And again it's trying to learn good practice from the retail sector. If you go into any supermarket, you will find certain commodities that are put into specific places; and that isn't random.... There's a huge amount of research and a huge amount of psychology that sits behind that, you'll get a good visual display on fruit and vegetables, you'll always find them given a fairly high priority. Quite often you'll find the bakery with its smells somewhere central to draw you in.'

This idea of linchpin stalls to serve as focal points was particularly evident in the former Islington farmers' market site, where the lamb-burger stall attracted large numbers into the market by abutting the edge of the pavement on which people walked past. Similarly, the fruit and vegetable stalls at the front of the Rotherham market appeared to be a significant attraction.

## Locational and physical attributes

### Proximity to town centre and transport links

Historically, markets were usually located in the centre of a town, typically in a square – the market square – surrounded by shops, and sometimes incorporating a covered area. This, too, is the European model. In many towns, the market would have been the main place in which locals shopped. In smaller towns and cities, town centres or market squares have remained the most common site for the market, although over the past two decades there has been a shift. In London, street markets both in residential areas and high streets have been the more common form.

What represents an optimal location, however, is difficult to determine. As Kris Zasada (Manchester market) puts it: 'In simple terms it is a question of does that market work for the location? And that's then subdivided into issues such as accessibility, the physical environment, critical mass ... and does it have a sense of place, which is extremely difficult to define.'

The extent to which a town centre site is beneficial for a market is a complex question. Although in the walking city of earlier centuries, such a site was optimal, with the growth of towns and cities and the increasing importance of parking, access to transport and other retail facilities, a town centre site can, if not well integrated into the wider shopping environment and other facilities, be problematic.

The complexities of locational attributes and the role they play is illustrated in Ludlow, which is poorly located in relation to wider shopping facilities, but the site itself, according to the market manager 'couldn't be better ... what makes it work really well is the position

Photo: David Studdert

Street entrance to St Mary's Market, St Helens

right at the centre of the town. You have the castle, the medieval shop, something like 180 listed buildings'. Certainly, for tourists the site is ideal, because they can combine a trip to the market with a visit to key adjacent local sites, such as the castle, although recent changes to parking regulations have barred coaches from parking outside the castle, with apparently detrimental effects on the numbers of tourists visiting the market. Nevertheless, its central location, well served by buses, was frequently praised by interviewees.

In Lowestoft, the site of the market, which is thoroughly integrated into the town's main shopping street and centre, and close to public transport and parking, meant that the majority of people shopping in the town passed through the market at some point during their visit. By contrast, in St Helens, the shift of the market to the edge of town from an earlier central position, which all the interviewees preferred, was reported to have had seriously detrimental effects on the market:

> 'I took our people to look at other markets. We decided that the magic ingredient for a market is car parking, bus services, access and footfall. I took them to a place like Bury market where, you know, trams come in, the bus station's next door. I've been to Leeds market on numerous occasions. The bus station is at the bottom. People feed off the buses. I took them to Widnes market. It is a good market because it's a council-built market, that one. Obviously they've got free car parking there, and bus services going past.... Your traditional market shopper used to pick the bus up next to the market which was where the bus station was. So traditionally, if you look at those markets which haven't changed, the bus station is always next to the market.' (St Helens, manager)

> 'We've got a front market here that nobody wants to go to … a brand new market … It's dead. The developer's architect built the pavement and the one-way system and took away the parking. No traffic comes down this way any more. There's no bloodline anymore. There's no reason for people to come down here. The bus station should always have been built at this site. I also believe a market should be in the centre of town. This is on the edge, and it makes a big difference. A market is the heart of a community and it should be built in the

centre. The bus station should have been built on this side so that people flowed through.' (St Helens, trader for more than 20 years)

The evidence from each of the markets pointed to a high degree of dependence on public transport by market shoppers, and an appreciation of the fact that in a number of markets – for example, Milton Keynes and Rotherham – there were nearby buses to take them home. Central town locations are likely to be well served by public transport and, for this reason alone, appeared to make market sites more viable.

## Parking provision

The provision of parking near to a market was also seen as a key issue by both traders and shoppers. For the former group, unloading vans in the morning necessitates easy access to the site. In Ridley Road, traders described being issued with parking tickets while unloading produce. Given that many people choose to shop in a market for fresh vegetables, fruit and other heavy goods, walking long distances to the car, particularly for women with children in tow or older people, may not be an option. This was an issue frequently cited in the interviews.

In Ludlow, for example, parking was seen as a major problem by shoppers because of the recent introduction of yellow lines, and by traders because of the fact that the coaches were now unable to park. In Ridley Road, too, despite its good location in relation to public transport, car parking was frequently cited as a major issue:

'Parking is shit! That's what's killed the market … there is nowhere to park at all.' (Ridley Road, trader)

'As the years have gone by, it has got steadily worse. So many people come shopping just to pick up a few cheap bits off the wall.… They used to be able to park all the way along here.… Now they go somewhere else.' (Ridley Road, trader)

'They don't come down here any more. The last time they came they parked, went and did a bit of shopping, and got a £120 wheel clamp on the car. You're not gonna see that person down here again.'(Ridley Road, trader)

However, there is often a conflict of views between market users, shoppers and traders, and the council with respect to parking. One key informant, Nick Rhodes (Leicester, market manager), pointed out, in his city: 'Well, the traders would like to see more parking, and they'd like to see parking closer to the market and that's the tension in itself; they want to see more parking and the council want to see more pedestrianisation.'

## Layout of market site

From the interviews with key informants, traders and shoppers, the physical shape of the market was revealed to be a significant factor in a market's success as a social space. As Graham Wilson of the National Asociation of British Markets Authorities (NABMA) commented: 'Markets are very much about interaction between traders and the public and design and space must promote and encourage this interaction.'

Markets that combined indoor and outdoor areas appeared to work well. In the traditionally English indoor and outdoor market of Rotherham, shoppers and traders were positive about the physical environment of the two markets, which combined a warm, well-lit inner space with a well-covered, atmospheric outdoor area. Nevertheless, there were some complaints:

> 'The roof leaks from the top, it gets wet in the aisles. Obviously, you know, your old aged pensioner could slip, hurt their ankles and so on. There's also quite a big hefty step to get onto here. This means we are unable to build a ramp for disabled access … which is a requirement that I think should be imposed within the market areas.' (Rotherham, trader)

One of the main reasons that the combination of outdoor and indoor markets was seen as a success was the fact that in poor weather conditions, shopping outside was not seen as appealing by shoppers, while at the same time making for unpleasant working conditions for the traders. The poor British climate is inevitably an inhibiting factor for successful outdoor social interaction over any extended period, and markets are no exception. For example, this female shopper in Ludlow said: 'I think there needs to be some better weather protection. I've seen people drenched before now because the water has pooled. The other day the wind blew and it just emptied completely over a little girl. I think they could erect some sort of covering.'

For this reason, indoor markets are popular with shoppers and, according to the traders and site managers interviewed, often have higher footfall than outdoor markets, during the winter months especially. A survey in Manchester supports this view. As Kris Zasada (market manager) reported: 'Once we accepted that we needed to redevelop the market, we tested that with the local shoppers, and about 95% of the people we asked said they would like weather protection for the new market.'

In Ludlow, many shoppers preferred the old covered market for the protection it offered from the weather. In this site, shoppers described being put off making a visit to the

*Photo: Sophie Watson*

Lowestoft market

market in bad weather. Certainly, on winter days during the research, particularly in the early part of the week, the market had a very sparse population, and social interaction was minimal. Similarly, in Preston:

'Today it's lovely. I'm sitting here getting a suntan. But in the winter, if you're on the edge, the wind blows in and if it's raining the wind carries the rain into the market. And it puts people off looking round and browsing. They come into the market at one end and they shoot through. I know they have to keep it open to keep the air pressure for the roof right. They should have given us some lightweight blinds. On a cold windy day you could drop them to maybe six foot high, which would be enough to stop the rain coming into the market. But they don't seem willing to spend any money. They'd rather paint the ironwork … than put the money into something more practical.' (Preston, trader)

In Lowestoft, the regeneration of the market had solved the problem by providing cheerfully painted shutters so that stallholders could leave their products locked up overnight, with, according to the traders, an apparent increase in people visiting the market:

'They will have all the rainwater guttering and everything that goes with it and security, sprinklers etc.… I think you'll find they are pretty bright … and there is lots of art work stencilled onto them … as you say, it is about bringing social vibrancy back to the area. It draws in staggering numbers … not just to the market but to the library, and to the other shops around here … I think it's around 17,000.' (Sunrise regeneration coordinator)

Another aspect to the layout of a market, as mentioned in the previous chapter, is the availability of seating, the lack of which was a frequent complaint made by several respondents in Milton Keynes: 'Yeah, there is nowhere to sit actually, there is nowhere to sit at all. So if you want to eat something you've got to buy it and walk off and find somewhere else to sit' (Milton Keynes, male, 41).

In summer, the stallholders put plastic seats out, which are well used, but during winter months shoppers tend to go to the shopping centre to sit down, because lack of cover in the market, where the water drips down off the flyover, was cited as a deterrent to staying in one place.

In Preston and Rotherham, pensioners sit on the benches provided in the indoor market for hours on end, and once a space is vacated it is soon filled up. As pointed out in Chapter 3, seating is considered particularly vital for older people. For example, two older female shoppers interviewed in St Helens said:

'We used to have an open market there and another market at this end that dates from the 1800s. What did St Helens do? They smashed the lot down and they built a monstrosity in their place. We don't like it. A lot of our generation don't like it. You know, there's not enough seats for people to sit down on. Old people want to sit and have a break and have a rest.'

The provision of seating represents another complex issue, however. The reluctance by councils to provide seating stems from a number of sources. Key informant Nick Rhodes (Leicester market) gave one reason: 'We were a bit sceptical about public seating because we thought the alcoholics are just going to sit there and we're going to have to kick them off every morning, but to be fair it's been used for the right reasons.'

Formal seating, though, does not guarantee social success, and creative and informal responses to its lack can be found in many markets that produce a more casual and relaxed sense of sociability and vibrancy. Ridley Road is one such classic example, where people were seen to sit for hours on packing cases, steps to the containers and walls. But for older or frail people, this is less of an option.

The more general environment of the market represents another part of the picture. If a market looks attractive in terms of the arrangement of the stalls, the distance between them, and an attractive display of goods, people are more likely to pass through the space, stop, look and chat. Where a market is clean, with no rubbish flying around in the wind or banana peels to slip on, it is also more likely to be more appealing to customers. Simon Quin of the Towns Centre Initiative noted in discussion of what issues matter for markets that in many of the ones that he had visited '… the stalls are too close together … and in some there's rats around the place and in the evening after the markets have finished no one's cleared the stuff away.'

In the research sites, however, ambivalent responses were given on the questions of cleanliness and the condition of the site. On the one hand, shabby conditions can be seen as off-putting, as shoppers reported on several occasions in Milton Keynes:

'I suppose that going through the market, it doesn't often stop us and say, you know, here's something I want; because it smells pretty appalling, kind of hamburgery, hot-doggy smells all over the place, different loud music and prices that seem unbelievably cheap. So that's the kind of middle-class prejudice that says that's so cheap it can't be good value…. I think it's highly accessible but it's not a particularly pleasant place to be.' (Milton Keynes, white male, 59)

(And in Preston:) 'Look in the middle there, how filthy it is. If they put a clear Perspex there it would bring some light in and brighten the place up.' (Preston, trader)

'The market is upstairs. And there are often problems with the escalators. Some of the old people can't walk up the stairs and the escalators keep breaking down.' (Preston, trader)

(And in St Helens:) 'The stalls are an old type, like what they used to be years ago. When you walk down that end, it's a bit cramped and dark, and not very inviting to people. When you come in this side it is very spacious and open and bright … but unfortunately there's no stalls.' (St Helens, market assistant)

These comments suggest that cleanliness and an attractive design and layout matter. On the other hand, in Ridley Road, the messy, dirty, ramshackle sense of the place was never commented on and seemed even to enhance the sense of the space as a lively one. It could be that the colourfulness of the stalls and people in the market offset any sense of shabbiness in this site.

Another issue is the overall layout of the site and how it fits in with its immediate environs; visibility and permeability are relevant here. The St Helens newly developed market suffered in this respect. The new front of the St Helens redeveloped market building looked out onto a little-used road where one bus stopped on its way out of town, opposite the Pilkington Glass museum, whose visitors – according to the curator – rarely crossed the road to the market. Entering from this direction, the empty stalls created a dead space.

If the market is not visible to people passing close by, it is unlikely to attract new shoppers, newcomers to the locality or tourists who may be less familiar with the area. Key informant George Nicholson (Borough Market) emphasised the importance of permeability:

> 'I think ... a sign of a good market is how permeable it is.... When Borough was a wholesale market, it was empty anyway but it just happened to have a crossroads in the middle of the city which is a vastly good place for a market....The one that's in the Arndale shopping centre (Manchester), which is built on the site of the old market tragically, but on the second floor of the Arndale ... it doesn't have any permeability. You go in, actually you can go out the other end on that one but it doesn't have the kind of openness that you associate with social space. In fact, I think probably the way the spaces are designed you can almost see whether they are social spaces, because that's just a box, a concrete box with an entrance. I think it's quite difficult to see how things are packed in, how you're going to get social space out of that because there's a reduced amount of opportunity for interaction. You know you go in and basically you buy or you don't, or you walk around and you might bump into someone but [you may not], so I think they're quite complex spaces – markets – but part of it's to do with the physical design.'

When the Islington farmers' market was moved to a school playground down a side street away from its prominent position on a pavement opposite Islington Green in a busy thoroughfare, the traders expressed concern that the lack of visibility would affect the market. Interestingly, as a result of good promotion of the market by LFM, the initial shortfall in visitors was beginning to fall off within three months, indicating that lack of visibility can be tackled where there is a will to do so.

A further key issue in the design of a market is the accessibility into, and through, the market for people in wheelchairs and people with pushchairs. The width of the aisles between the stalls is the main issue here. In Lowestoft, where the aisles were relatively wide, people in wheelchairs were a frequent sight, although the social atmosphere of the market was relatively low key, while in the outdoor Preston market, where there are wide aisles, pensioners could be seen stopping and chatting throughout the day. Once again though, this issue, and its relation to vibrancy and social interaction, is not entirely clear-cut. In Rotherham, where some of the aisles were quite narrow, and in Ridley Road, where the walking area between the two rows of stalls along the road's edge is relatively narrow, the markets were both teaming with shoppers who stopped to chat, look at the produce and bargain with the traders, creating an atmosphere of buzz and vitality, which can be lacking in more spaciously laid out markets.

Finally, the safety and security of a market space is another issue of concern – whether a site feels threatening and is poorly lit. This was an issue raised by women as a deterrent, in a number of sites, particularly the more dilapidated older markets.

## Relation to other retail outlets and customer facilities

The question of a market's proximity, or not, to other retail outlets, particularly supermarkets, is a vexed one. On the one hand, markets need to be integrated into the wider shopping environment, so that shoppers can combine market shopping with other shopping activity, which may include shopping in a nearby supermarket for goods that are not available in the local market. On the other hand, if a supermarket is located at some distance from a market, and parking is provided, it may attract shoppers away from the local market, because of ease of parking and longer shopping hours along with other factors, such as the cheapness of products, the wider range, quality control and the possibility of returning damaged goods.

In Lowestoft and St Helens, the market and shopping centre were so closely linked that the identities of the two were intertwined and shoppers moved from one to the other comparing prices and products, in some cases to the market's disadvantage. On the other hand, the closure of the supermarket Kwiksave on the market square in Ludlow was universally seen to have had a negative impact on footfall in the market, particularly among older shoppers who had combined supermarket and market shopping in the same site. In Milton Keynes market, which is adjacent to a large shopping centre,

*Photo: Sophie Watson*

Market at rear of Britten shopping centre, Lowestoft

*Photo: Sophie Watson*

Milton Keynes market, viewed from shopping centre

customers to the market, particularly in the winter, reported restricting their activity in the market to shopping and returning to the indoor shopping centre to meet their friends and have coffee or a meal, thereby diminishing the role of the market for social interaction.

This last point relates to one of the crucial elements revealed in the research for a market to work as a social space, which is the location of a café, or other food outlets such as a food or tea van, or a pub in the market site. Where these are absent or minimal, such as in Ludlow, the time spent in the market site is notably less. Islington farmers' market is an exception, which can be explained by the commitment to tasting food and discussing produce with traders, and the custom of putting out samples for shoppers to try. In Rotherham, the café in the market site was full at all times of the day, as was the van at the top, and Ridley Road market stalls sold tea, coffee and an array of different foods, including goat curry. Outdoor vans and cafés, not surprisingly, were little patronised in cold or bad weather – for example, in markets like Lowestoft, where the café has outdoor seats adjacent to the market, a notably diminished level of social interaction was evident in winter months.

Of importance, also, in attracting and keeping people in the market site is the presence of public facilities such as a post office, advice centres – as in Rotherham – and toilets, the lack of which was mentioned in a number of sites including Ridley Road and Ludlow. In Preston, for example, the closure of a post office was reported to have had a very detrimental effect on the market:

> 'This used to be the hub of the town centre. We had the post office over there which is now closed and gone down Fishergate.' (Preston, trader)

> 'There's definitely less people coming through since they closed the post office.' (Preston, trader)

As Kris Zasada (market manager) put it: 'Again, it's about customer service. Do they have access to toilets, is there a catering offer there, are there changing rooms? Because that's a real challenge on street markets, where you've got lots of sales of clothing.'

## Management and planning of markets

*Vision, strategy and plans in local markets*

Many respondents, particularly among the key informants and traders, described a lack of interest in markets by many local authorities. Although the provision of markets expanded in the 1980s to raise revenue, in many localities there has been a subsequent lack of investment or strategic thinking on the role of the local market, and interviewees referred to 'old-fashioned attitudes'. Graham Wilson (NABMA) for example, noted that: 'Markets are not viewed by local authorities as a front-line service. There is some movement particularly in respect of authorities where partnership schemes are being promoted and PPS 6 [*Planning Policy Statment 6*; ODPM 2005] gives us some governmental encouragement.'

According to this respondent, there are some market authorities and companies running markets such as Borough Market and those in Belfast, Leicester, Bradford, Bury and Manchester that provide good examples because they have thought 'outside the box' and been innovative in the way they have promoted their markets. They have also managed to obtain investment.

Simon Quin (Towns Centre Initiative) reinforced the point:

'I think they were just seen as a cash cow for local authorities, like car parks, and there was no real investment, in fact; and gradually (by the late nineties) they were seen as actually not making as much money as they used to and what's going to happen in the future, and what are all these issues that we've got to deal with?'

In St Helens, disappointment at council neglect was consistently expressed:

'The council has a Cinderella syndrome about markets. They are interested in the income we produce and they want us to be financially viable. Once you get to a position where they are no longer financially viable, markets close or get relocated, or sections get sold off. In my view, there is no great interest in markets from councillors and elected members because we are not what you would call a traditional market town.' (St Helens, manager)

Markets are frequently managed by the property section or the treasurer's department in the council, within a much bigger empire where the chief officer has a huge span of issues to consider, and where they are accountable to a member with a vast portfolio, so 'they rarely appear either on the political radar or the officer radar' (George Nicholson, Borough Market). The impact of a lack of strategic thinking on markets is felt most acutely by the traders, and little commented on by shoppers, but a lack of vision and strategy has an impact on other issues discussed here that enhance the value of a market as social space. This was very evident in the case of Islington farmers' market, which is run by a very proactive and forward-thinking company. When the market was relocated, for example, LFM had assiduously promoted the new site in the local media and adjacent neighbourhood.

The market managers represented the more visible face of the council, and were frequently mentioned in the interviews as having a significant effect on the markets, particularly the lives of the traders. The market manager at Ludlow, for example, was highly visible on the market site on most days, and had a seemingly very positive relationship with traders:

'I've got a job and they are making a living. I do no end of little favours for them. If their car is in for service, I pick them up from the garage … and they do the same for me.… I wouldn't do the job unless I knew the traders liked me and I liked them too.' (Ludlow, market manager).

Similarly, in Lowestoft: 'Bob who is here all the time, bless him, he works his socks off. Any problems, he will deal with it' (Lowestoft, trader).

However, responses in Milton Keynes were far more mixed, from 'You get a bin bag if you're lucky. The rubbish sometimes gets collected sometimes doesn't' (Milton Keynes, trader) to 'Nothing's too much you know, you got any complaints, you talk to them about it. They're always nice, they'll do what they can to help you out, they're really, really good blokes, yeah' (Milton Keynes, trader).

Uncertainty as to the market's future seemed to have significantly undermined Preston market, and traders and shoppers alike referred to the possibility of its imminent demise: 'Well, they're closing it down, aren't they? They're trying to run it down … they are going to flatten this and enclose the market, to box it all in and so all this will disappear' (Preston, shopper).

A trader in the market told his story:

'They kept pushing the same proposal around. And then they had a feasibility study and spent £20,000 on that. Nothing ever gets done. So we got absolutely sick and fed up of it. We just said, we may as well buy it. The council couldn't borrow any money.... So it was a case of, if we didn't do it ourselves, nothing would get done.... We got to the end of it and then, hey presto, they started to stall on whether they would sign it over to us.... And then we found out that Grosvenor were interested.... The first we knew about it. There was a town centre initiative meeting 12 months before we got to the end of our date of borrowing ... and all parties were invited to turn up. We all sat there and drew pretty pictures on pieces of paper in groups of four. I didn't know that one of these groups of four was Grosvenor. But that was two years down the line. We'd been at it for two years by then.... So when we got to the end and said, you know, cards on the table, why aren't we signing up?, somebody said, Grosvenor are interested in all of the town centre and your proposal is only for the market. Our proposal was that we would have bought this place.' (Preston, trader)

However, it is not always easy to ensure that council staff dealing with markets are well versed in the particular issues of concern. Managing a market site can be an unfamiliar portfolio, which may be grouped alongside parking and estate management. This situation is not helped by the lack of professional training for market managers, who come from a variety of backgrounds, often unrelated to the needs of market management.

Kris Zasada (Manchester market) commented:

'I think there is a real issue within our industry that we don't have a professional body that provides and maintains the professional standards and qualifications that are needed ... lots of people drift into market management from different areas of local government, and there isn't much of a national process to enable them to learn all the skills that are required.'

If the market site is run well and for the optimum length of time each day, which may vary according to the needs of the local population, it seems more likely to succeed as a social space. There was a prevalent view that there were currently too many markets and too many market days. Graham Wilson (NABMA) put it this way:

'The expansion in the 1980s and early 1990s was handled badly. Markets were seen as an income generator and the money propped up mainstream services such as education and there was no investment from profits.... Lack of government recognition and poor planning policies have also had an impact.'

There are clear implications for social interaction here because, if the people inclined to shop in markets are spread too thinly over too many sites, the vibrancy and social life of a market suffers. In most of the markets in the study, the market was much emptier in the earlier part of the week, with consequently less social interaction on the site.

Shoppers in the markets with a higher stall vacancy rate commented on the fact that this created a negative impression and a sense of failure: 'Because there's a lot of empty stalls I don't think it encourages people to come in, they don't see a bustling market atmosphere, you see, which you do in other markets. People come for the atmosphere. They don't like it when it's empty' (St Helens, trader).

This concern was not evident in markets with lower vacancies, such as Ludlow or Islington farmers' market.

## Promotion and marketing

Promotion is a key issue for markets. Widespread local knowledge of the site, and the hours and days of opening, were reported by traders as vital to a market's success. This is particularly the case when a market is shifted to a new site, as in Islington, or redeveloped, as in Lowestoft:

> 'It is, they tend to stay here and talk, which is really nice because then you have time to talk to people who sell, the farmers and everything else. Whereas before the aisles were very small, two or three feet wide, they didn't have time to speak to anybody. We don't obviously get the passing trade, the bus doesn't stop outside, but apart from that, as long as the advertising stays up and the boards are out on the street, then it should be fine.' (Interviewee)

## Conclusion

In this chapter, we have argued that there are a number of ingredients that play a significant role in making a market both socially viable and, at best, thriving. The relationship between the economic viability of a market and its success as a social space is not easy to disentangle, because the fact that a market is thriving economically does not ensure that it is a space where shoppers will stop and chat, engage with others or form social connections, although some sense of economic success is necessary to underpin the effective operation of sites as commercial entities. Dwell time in the market is an important factor in creating the conditions for people to engage with others and this appears to be influenced by a number of factors, which include products that match the community's needs at reasonable prices, a pleasant environment to linger in, seating, cafés or other eating outlets as a focal point and a buzzy atmosphere to attract people in.

The following tables have been constructed to elucidate some of the differences between the markets and come to some conclusions as to the importance of various attributes for the success of market sites as public spaces for social interaction, social mixing or social inclusion. The assessment of a market's atmosphere and sociability brought together first impressions recorded at the start of the research and observations made across the study period. All the markets were quieter in the early part of the week and also during the winter months. However, the level of use, and therefore the overall atmosphere of the market, varied far less across the seasons where the market was indoors, as in St Helens, or contained an indoor site, as in Rotherham. Notwithstanding these daily and seasonal variations, fairly clear overall summary descriptions of each market's atmosphere can confidently be offered.

**Table 4.1: Economic and management attributes of the markets**

| Factor | Ridley Road | Lowestoft | St Helens | Milton Keynes | Islington | Ludlow | Preston | Rotherham |
|---|---|---|---|---|---|---|---|---|
| Level of mixed use in retail offer | Good mix of stalls, eating outlets, adjacent shops. | Site adjacent to other shopping outlets, community facilities and café. | Café only site breaking up market space. | Predominantly a shopping space. | Predominantly a shopping space. | Central town ties it in with nearby shopping and eating activities. | Predominantly a shopping space combined with good café provision. | Very mixed-use space, including more established retail outlets, bordering on community facilities, advice centres, and cafés. |
| Range and quality of goods | Ethnic diversity. Good-quality, good-value food and household products. | Limited daily range but good coverage on market days. | Very limited range. No fresh produce except meat. Cheap, low quality. | Diverse and wide range of cheap products. | Very high-quality and diverse range of fresh produce. High prices. | Very high-quality local food, craft and tourist items. | Good quality, variety of food and other products. | Very diverse range of food products and goods. Good value. |
| Management | Limited on-site management. | Strong on-site management. | Strong on-site management. | Private company management, mixed input. | Active on-site manager. | Strong on-site management. | Variable on-site management. | Strong on-site management. |
| Vision | No council vision. | Strong vision from local regeneration project. Limited local council vision. | Very limited council vision. | Limited council vision. | Strong LFM vision for market. | Interested and positive council vision. | Limited council vision. High levels of uncertainty regarding market's future. | Strong council support. |
| Unique selling point | Ethnically diverse products. | Not apparent | Not apparent | Very wide range of low-cost products | Fresh organic food. | Crafts and fresh local produce. | Good site and wide range of products. | Excellent central location well connected to local community centres and cafés. |

**Table 4.2: Locational and physical attributes of the markets**

| Key factors | Ridley Road | Lowestoft | St Helens | Milton Keynes | Islington | Ludlow | Preston | Rotherham |
|---|---|---|---|---|---|---|---|---|
| **Access to public transport** | Good. No close underground. National rail more than 50 yards. 9 buses within 70 yards. No taxi ranks. | Good. National rail 250 yards. Within 200 yards of the market buses serving Lowestoft and towns within region. Taxi rank 200 yards. | Some problems. National rail 0.5 miles away. Main entrance served by one bus stop. Main city bus station 250 yards in other direction. Taxi rank 100 yards. | Good. National rail 9 miles away. Very good bus service both sides of market serving town and surrounding area. Taxi rank 100 yards. | Adequate. Undergrounds at 0.45 miles and 0.7 miles. British Rail 0.22 miles away. 8 buses from 0.15 to 0.25 miles away. | Adequate. National rail with limited services 0.75 miles away at bottom of hill on which market sits. No bus station, but bus pick-up and drop-off point 50 yards away serving Ludlow and other local towns. No dedicated taxi rank. | Good. National rail 660 yards from market. Major bus station 125 yards away through St John's shopping centre. Serves Preston and surrounding region. 80 yards from bus stop serving serving destinations within Preston area. | Good. National rail 0.5 miles away. Substantial bus station 200/300 yards from market- hub for local and regional bus services. Dedicated taxi rank 250 yards away. |
| **Parking** | Poor. Limited pay and display, £1.20– £2 per hr. Majority resident or business parking in surrounding areas. Active parking attendant presence. | Good. Minimal accessible on- street parking. Adjacent multi-storey car park 650 places. 1 hr 55p; 4 hrs £2.20; all day £2.75. | Good. Multi- storey car park by foot through adjacent shopping centre. 0.5 hrs 20p; 1hr 60p; 2hrs £1; 3 hrs £2; 3+ hrs £4. Other multi-storey car parks nearby. No street parking near front entrance. | Good. Multi- storey parking. (550 spaces). Free. Open-air parking £1 up to 2 hrs and some free parking up to 2 hrs. | Adequate. No car parks in vicinity but no restrictions on on-street parking on Sundays. | Poor. Limited on- street parking. Small car park (28 spaces) 10 yards away. Free. Max stay 1 hr. Further down hill, more free parking and 6 disabled parking bays. Small open- air car park 100 yards away: 30p 1 hr; 80p up to 3hrs. | Good. Multi- storey car park, 10 levels. £1 per hr; 5+ hrs £8. Disabled parking spaces close to market. Shopmobility scheme 300 yards from market. Limited street pay and display. | Good. Large covered market above bus station 250 yards away. 1hr 60p; 2 hrs 80p; 3 hrs £1.20; 4 hrs £1.60; 5 hrs £2.50; all day £4. Parking bays for traders; access at start of day, later available to holders of disabled badges. Limited on-street parking. |

(continued)

**Table 4.2: Locational and physical attributes (continued)**

| Key factors | Ridley Road | Lowestoft | St Helens | Milton Keynes | Islington | Ludlow | Preston | Rotherham |
|---|---|---|---|---|---|---|---|---|
| **Layout of market site** | Crowded street market spilling into surrounding area. | Small enclosed site with limited number of stalls. | New building poorly arranged. | Outdoor, adjacent to large shopping centre. Close to flyover. | Outdoor in school playground. Away from main street. | Outdoor. In town centre near castle. | Outdoor. 2 sections. Indoor. 2 storeys. Close to town centre. | Outdoor and indoor. 2 storeys. Close to town centre. |
| **Links with other retail outlets** | Close to high street and shopping centre. | Close to high street and shopping centre. | In large shopping centre but at far end of smallest mall. | Adjacent to shopping centre. | At a distance from other shops. | At a distance from supermarket. | Integrated into large shopping area and centres. | Short distance to other shops. |
| **Visibility from outside** | Good. | Not easy to see from main high street. | Very poor. | Poor. | Good temporary signage from Upper St, none on other proximate streets. | Good. | Good signage on roads. | Good. |
| **Links with amenities and local resources** | Weak. | Next to public library. | Weak. | Weak. | Weak. | Weak. | Post office recently closed. | Next to advice and referral centres. |
| **Cafés and food vans** | Café. Food vans on site. | Nearby café. No food van. | Café. | No café. Food vans. | No café. Lamb-burger stall. | Tea rooms nearby. Food van on site. | Several cafés close by. Pub open from 10.30am, well-used all day. | 3 cafés and food vans on site. |

Table 3: Social attributes of the markets

| Attributes | Ridley Road | Lowestoft | St Helens | Milton Keynes | Islington | Ludlow | Preston | Rotherham |
|---|---|---|---|---|---|---|---|---|
| Atmosphere | Very vibrant, busy, noisy, scruffy, informal. Endless chatter. | Low-key, quiet space, but constant stream of people passing through. | Very quiet and empty, down-at-heel feel. | Busy but rather dowdy/scruffy feel. | Busy and cheerful, bright, affluent. | Bustle and movement. Typical country-market feel. | On lower floors and outside, busy and sociable. Empty upstairs. | Very vibrant. Packed and cheerful. |
| Buzz index 1–6 (6 = high) | 6 | 2 | 1 | 2 | 5 | 5 | 4 | 4 |
| Social interaction | Very high level of social interaction across all groups. | Some lingering at stalls, particularly make-up and books stalls. | Café is sole social space. | Low-key daily interactions. | Lots of meeting and chat between friend and acquaintances. Groups forming and reforming. | High levels of social interaction between families and friends. | Good levels of day-to-day social interaction. | Good levels of daily social interaction. Lots of chat and clustering in pairs and groups. |
| Social mixing | Strong connections between traders of different ethnicities and customers. | Social contact between young and old within families. | Very limited. | Limited mixing across ethnic/age groups. | Mainly middle-class clientèle but mixed age. | Social mixing across different age groups. | Limited interracial/ethnic mixing. | Good connections across age groups but reported interracial tension. |
| Social inclusion | Strong focal point for local low-income and mixed-race community. | Frequented by wheelchair users and older people. | Frequented by older people, wheelchair users, and very young single mothers. | Used by lower-income groups in local community. | Limited inclusion of local low-income or ethnically diverse groups. | Very inclusive of local homogeneous community. | Inclusive of local working-class community. | Very important to local pensioner community. |

In summary, for a market to exist as a social space, there are several basic requirements. First, a good range of products that match what the local community is looking to buy is the single most important requirement for a market to work both economically and socially. Thus the social and economic aspects of market are intertwined. Second, people need to get to a market – both public transport and/or good parking access is important. In particular, negative features such as parking problems act as a clear deterrent to shoppers visiting and spending time in the market. Third, the presence of cafés and food vans, and informal and formal seating on site, enhance opportunities for just sitting, at the very least, or more extended social interaction. Fourth, although good management is not crucial for a market to function well as a social space, with the exception of Ridley Road, the markets that appeared to be most vibrant and social were also those where positive comments about the practices of the market manager in particular, and also the strategies of the council, were frequently made. The traders also clearly play a crucial role in attracting people into the social life of the market, and more established traders appear to be more comfortable in this role. The links between the social and economic aspects of a market are once again paramount here because, if traders are not making a decent income, they will withdraw from that site to a more profitable market or leave the trade.

Returning to the earlier tables, there is considerable variation in the social roles played by the markets in the study. At one end of the continuum, Ridley Road exhibited high levels of social interaction, social mixing, social bonding and social inclusion, even though parking access was poor and there was no council strategy for the site. The diversity of products, the strong trader presence and the good public transport links were strong factors in the market's success. Strong social ties were also evident in Ludlow, Rotherham and Preston, where long-standing trader families in the market provided an important focus for the local community. Lowestoft appeared to play a less active role as a social space, despite the good access to public transport and parking and strong links with the local shopping centre and library. Here, there was insufficient buzz and activity in the market, and limited social space to draw people in and encourage them to stay. St Helens had few attributes to draw people into the market. Its prime social function was as a site of social inclusion, the café at the centre of the market operating as a popular social space for those more marginalised in the wider community, and the cheapness of some goods (though lacking fresh produce apart from meat) drawing some householders, notably young single mothers, into the market.

The attractive food products at Islington clearly attracted a particular section of the local community – the middle classes – who enjoyed social interaction in that space, although dwell time was limited by the lack of provision of a café or major food outlets on site. The high prices meant that this market did not really operate as a site of social mixing or social inclusion. Similarly Ludlow, although also more middle class in its clientèle due to the town's local socioeconomic profile, attracted a broader community, with its good local produce at reasonable prices, good location, access to public transport, well-managed site and proximity to tea shops. The parking problems at this site nevertheless deterred some customers from shopping in this market. Rotherham market demonstrated the value of strong locational and physical attributes combined with good economic/management attributes, low-cost and good-quality products, and a buzzy atmosphere, thus overall providing a strong site of social interaction as well as an inclusive space for the local community. Preston was similarly buzzy, with high levels of daily social interaction, its only real difference from Rotherham being the uncertainty around its future, which some traders and shoppers reported finding demoralising.

It is clear from this summary and the information presented in the tables that there is a complexity of interrelated factors that contribute to the success of a market as a social space, and which need consideration by local and national policy makers and practitioners.

# 5

# Conclusions and policy recommendations

'I'm not saying that investment is the be-all and end-all.... People have come to me and said, you need to put a new floor in, you need to do this, that and the other. And I've been to some of the grottiest markets possible, but they are the busiest.... And I have been to markets which have spent millions of pounds on the flooring, and new escalators and you name it, and it's made no difference.' (Preston, council official)

Not surprisingly, the picture that emerges from this research into what makes markets successful spaces of social interaction and diversity is a complex and textured one. Although the markets in the study varied considerably in the level of social interaction, the strength of social ties, the level of social inclusion and the use of the market by different groups, in all the markets some degree of social interaction took place, and in most cases respondents confirmed the significance of the market as a social space. The research therefore concluded that all markets operate as social spaces, even if simply as a public space for marginalised members of the community to shop or pass the time of day. As such, they play a crucial, and mostly neglected, role in local communities.

Of the selected market sites, Rotherham, Ridley Road, Ludlow and Islington farmers' market were the ones where the highest levels of social interaction were observed. The populations visiting the first two were predominantly from low-income groups and, in the case of Ridley Road, more ethnically/racially mixed. Ridley Road represented the site of greatest social mixing. However, Milton Keynes and Preston markets also exhibited many instances of social interaction, and both these markets played a role in the social life of their local communities. The other two markets, Lowestoft and St Helens, while not being sites of much social interaction, appeared to play a social inclusion role in providing public spaces for marginalised groups to see others and spend time outside the home – St Helens was the most striking in this respect.

In all sites, the social relationships between shoppers and traders were relatively strong, and certain groups, particularly older people, clearly used the market as a meeting place or bumped casually into friends and acquaintances. Overall, the group for whom the market was most significant as a site of social interaction was older people, and women particularly, followed by families with children at the weekend and single parents with young children during the week. However, young people and younger/middle-aged adults without children were also visible in markets, particularly, in the case of the former, Rotherham market and, in the case of the latter, Islington farmers' market.

A number of attributes were found to contribute, in varying degrees, to the success of a market as a social space. Essential attributes were as follows:

- **features to attract visitors to the site** – including a diverse range of products that made a good 'fit' with local community needs and 'tastes', and a sense of surprise or the unexpected to provide interest;

- **opportunities to linger** – café(s) or food van(s) on site or close by were key here; informal seating areas could also be important, but less critical;
- **good access to the site** – public transport was key, but opportunities to come by car and access to parking were also important for some visitors;
- **an active and engaged community of traders** – both to provide the retail offer but also to provide part of the social life of the site itself.

Other important, but less essential, attributes were as follows:

- **a well laid out site** – with thought given to the layout of the stalls, linchpin stalls or features (the café often being one) and particular features such as roomy aisles for people to walk through easily, as well as protection from the weather in more open sites;
- **connection with other retail outlets** – to ensure that the market was embedded among local retail outlets;
- **effective management of the site** – including a leadership role from councils to provide a strategic direction for the market.

## National policy issues

Many respondents, particularly the key informants, commented on the lack of policy or strategy for markets at a national level. Markets could play a crucial role in helping to deliver many of the national government's agendas – especially those which concern healthy eating, sustainability, social cohesion and the building of communities. The lack of connection of these political priorities into policy on local markets represents a significant lost opportunity.

There are two current policy agendas in particular where opportunities for raising the profile of markets exist. The first of these is the social exclusion agenda. Core to this is the objective of creating sustainable, inclusive communities in towns, cities and rural areas. Programmes have focused on children and young people, crime, employment and opportunity, homes and neighbourhoods, and transport and development. Clearly, markets could play a crucial role in many of these initiatives; however, they have not formed a part of the policy agenda. Markets have the potential to provide key public spaces for the local communities to meet, including opportunities for children and young people, and the potential for employment generation and the testing of new products and ideas in a local site, as we saw with the young Rasta soap maker and trader in Ridley Road.

Town centre management initiatives and regeneration policies represent the second underexploited avenue for raising the profile of markets. Town centre management involves partnerships between private and public bodies – primarily local authorities, which contribute anything from 10-80% of the running costs – and local businesses. In Britain, there are now approximately 500 town centre managers. According to Simon Quin, Chief Executive of the Association of Town Centre Management, markets could play a key role in the regeneration and redevelopment of town centres, which in the majority of cases is missed. There are exceptions, such as Manchester, Norwich, Leicester, Bolton, Ilford and Romford, among others, where markets are recognised as part of the picture in local plans. In addition to this economic role, markets offer something more. Although the new PPS 6: *Planning for Town Centres* (ODPM, 2005) endorses the role of markets in making a valuable contribution to the vitality of town centres, as well as contributing to local choice and diversity in shopping, there is little emphasis on the role of markets as social and public spaces. Given the potential for markets to act as significant sites of social interaction and, perhaps to a lesser extent, of social mixing and inclusion in a community, their place in community development and local regeneration policies could be strengthened.

## Local policy issues

An important component of market strategy is responding to the sociodemographic profile of the locality, and ensuring that markets meet the needs of their population. At the economic level, this means encouraging into the market traders who meet the shopping needs and desires of the local community. One example of recent good practice is offered by the strategies employed by the Gospel Oak Neighbourhood Management Initiative, under the government's 2001 Neighbourhood Management Pathfinder Scheme for regenerating deprived areas. Here, in Queen's Crescent market, several new stalls were introduced in 2005-06, such as those selling organic bread and cakes, Italian cheeses and olives, fish and jewellery, and an Indian fresh food stall. These were to encourage new people back into an old inner London market that had been in decline for several years. The market has also been rebranded with the placement of new and brightly coloured stalls and shopping bags, and the parking issues that had contributed to the loss of several long-established traders are also being addressed. Initial observations indicate that the policy has been a success.

At the physical, infrastructural and locational level, a market strategy also needs to ensure that the market site is accessible, particularly to older people, people with disabilities and those with children, as well as providing a site that has good protection from the weather, seating, wide enough aisles and other attributes that attract customers to the market.

Some respondents noted that partnership arrangements were the best route for obtaining the investment that is required to build a market's infrastructure so that it can compete successfully. The involvement of market traders in the running of a market is another significant component. A specific strategy and vision for the market at council level is also key, as opposed to placing markets within a wider profile of activities, such as parking or estate management, where the market's potential role to contribute economically and socially to an area can be lost. At the site level, a well-trained and responsive market manager can make a real difference to the effective running of the market, and therefore to its success as a social space.

Given the evident success of farmers' markets, specialist markets such as Christmas markets, French and German markets, and Borough Market, similar provision in local areas should be encouraged. In this study, research at Islington farmers' market revealed the added significance of this market type as a social space, at least for the better-off members of the local community.

Most importantly, market provision in any one locality needs to fit with the surrounding community needs. Where a market is located in a predominantly low-income area, the provision of affordable, high-quality goods will draw large numbers of people into the site, and where there is good seating, cafés and high levels of accessibility, older people in particular will be encouraged to dwell for considerable lengths of time, as in Rotherham market. In contrast, where a market is located in an ethnically mixed area, to attract a wide diversity of customers into the market, the provision of a variety of food products, goods and even eating places that serve ethnically diverse food is essential in making a market a successful social space. Therefore, for a market to work, both economically and socially, it is crucial that the strategy and vision for a market at the local level needs to be sensitive to the local conditions and needs of the community in which it is situated.

# References

Bromley, R. (1998) 'Market place trading and the transformation of retail space in the expanding Latin American city', *Urban Studies*, vol 35, no 8.

Deutsche, R. (1996) *Evictions: Art and Spatial Politics*, Cambridge, MA: MIT Press.

Fincher, R. and Jacobs, J. (eds) (1998) *Cities of Difference*, New York, NY: Guilford Press.

Habermas, J. (1984) *The Theory of Communicative Action Vol. 1: Reason and the Rationalisation of Society*, London: Heinemann.

Kaznelson, I. (1981) *City Trenches: Urban Politics and Patterning of Class in the US*, New York, NY: Pantheon Books.

Massey, D., Allen, J. and Pile, S. (eds) (1999) *City Worlds*, London: Routledge.

Mitchell, D. (1995) 'The end of public space? People's Park, definitions of the public and democracy', *Annals of the Association of American Geographers*, vol 85, pp 108-33.

Mitchell, D. (2003) *The Right to the City*, New York, NY and London: Guilford Press.

ODPM (Office of the Deputy Prime Minister) (2003) *Living Places: Cleaner, Safer, Greener*, London: The Stationery Office.

ODPM (2005) *Planning Policy Statement 6: Planning for Town Centres*, London: The Stationery Office.

NABMA (National Association of British Markets Authorities) (2005) *National Retail Markets Survey*, Oswestry: NABMA.

Sennett, R. (1974) *The Fall of Public Man*, New York, NY: Norton.

Sennett, R. (2000) 'Reflections on the public realm', in G. Bridge and S. Watson (eds) *The Blackwell Companion to the City*, Oxford: Blackwell, p 380-88.

Sherry, J.F. (1990) 'A socio-cultural analysis of a mid-western flea market', *Journal of Consumer Research*, vol 17, June.

Simmel, G. (1903a) 'The metropolis and mental life', in G. Bridge and S. Watson (eds) (2002) *The Blackwell City Reader*, Oxford: Blackwell, pp 11-19.

Simmel, G. (1903b) 'On spatial projections of social forms', *Zeitschrift fur Sozialwissenschaft*, vol 6, pp 287-302.

Simmel, G. (1903c) 'Soziologie des raumes Jahrbruch', *Gesetzgebung, Verwaltung und Volkswirtschaft*, vol 27, pp 27-71.

Smith, N. (1996) *The New Urban Frontier: Gentrification and the Revanchist City*, London: Routledge.

Sorkin, M. (1992) *Variations on a Theme Park: The New American City and the End of Public Space*, New York, NY: Hill and Wong.

*The Economist* (2003) August 2, p 37.

Urban Task Force (1999) *Towards an Urban Renaissance* (the Richard Rogers report), London: The Stationery Office.

Watson, S. and Wells, K. (2005) 'Spaces of nostalgia: The hollowing out of a London market', *Journal of Social and Cultural Geography*, vol 6, no 6, pp 17-29.

Watson, S. (2006) *City Publics: The (Dis)enchantments of Urban Encounter*, London: Routledge.

Wells, K. and Watson, S. (2005) 'A politics of resentment: shopkeepers in a London neighbourhood', *Ethnic and Racial Studies*, vol 28, no 2, pp 261-77.

Young, I. (1990) *Justice and the Politics of Difference*, Princeton, NJ: Princeton University Press.